AF718180

The Unauthorised Bible

The Revelation of the Spirit

– J F EVANS –

An environmentally friendly book printed and bound in England by
www.printondemand-worldwide.com

Mixed Sources
Product group from well-managed forests, and other controlled sources
FSC www.fsc.org Cert no. TT-COC-002641
© 1996 Forest Stewardship Council

PEFC Certified
This product is from sustainably managed forests and controlled sources
PEFC PEFC/16-33-415 www.pefc.org

This book is made entirely of chain-of-custody materials

J F Evans

FastPrint Publishing

www.fast-print.net/store.php

The Unauthorised Bible – The Revelation of the Spirit

www.unathorisedbible.com

ISBN 978-178035-053-0

First published 2011 by
FASTPRINT PUBLISHING
Peterborough, England.

J F Evans

Introduction

This volume is actually the final chapter from a much larger endeavour which I have been working on for the last few years: the Unauthorised Bible, A Universal Scripture, which is an attempt to illustrate that most of the scriptures from the major world religions, in their original form, are all saying basically the same thing. It has also been constructed in order to hopefully demonstrate that the teachings of the orthodox established religions bear little relationship to the original teachings of their notional founders.

This concluding section stands on its own as my attempt to reconcile the traditional, or at least notional, conflict between religious establishments, the domain of faith, and scientific knowledge, the domain of the rational. It covers most of the great questions that have taxed humanity since whenever we became sentient, and is, therefore, not only a conclusion to the larger work, but also a justification.

Whether I have succeeded in such an impudent, and probably imprudent, undertaking is for others to determine, but I am presumptuous enough to think that I have found the solution to the questions that have been bothering me for forty odd years, and if my answers are of any assistance to others then my labours will have served a better purpose than just a personal quest.

This book does contain a political bias, as do all works of this kind, whether acknowledged or not, and mine are based around a love of freedom, without which moral responsibility is meaningless, and a belief that men and women are in terms of the spirit absolute and complete equals. Anyone who is wedded religiously to tradition, from whatever background they come from, reads on at their peril: they are likely to be thoroughly offended: but they have been warned.

Table of Contents

Acknowledgements

First to my mother, Audrey Evans, for teaching me to read and introducing me to the world of books, and for later bullying me into joining, against my better inclinations, that middle class marriage bureau that masqueraded as the youth wing of a much loved political party, and thereby effectively reintroducing me to the then young lady who was to become my wife, partner in life, best friend and soulmate.

To my teachers and tutors throughout my studies from primary school onwards, but most especially to the staff at the old Bridlington School, and particularly to Frank Thompson, Mike Mortimer, and John Hillditch, for inducting me respectively into the delights of physics, history, and philosophy.

To Michael Young, Jennie Lee, and Harold Wilson for creating the wonderful institution that is the Open University, without which I would have had no redemption from the academic wilderness, to which, through my own idleness, I had banished myself, and which channelled my studies into some sort of coherence.

To Kahlil Gibran for his seminal work The Prophet, which gave me the literary device, the template as it were, around which the ideas presented here could be put forward other than as an academic text, and, hopefully therefore, in a more 'user-friendly' style.

To the many modern authors whose works have introduced me to new ideas and concepts, and hopefully have expanded my own consciousness, but particularly Lyall Watson, James Lovelock, Darryl Reanney, Paul Davies, Peter Singer, Elaine Pagels, Neale Donald Walsch, Eckhart Tolle, Timothy Freke and Peter Gandy; and to the numerous theologians, scientists, philosophers and historians who have amplified, I think, my understanding.

To the numerous relatives and friends and colleagues who, throughout my sojourn through life and experience, be it business, schools and colleges, church, politics, clubs and societies, have contributed, even be it unknowingly, to driving me or leading me, by and through their tolerating my obsessive need to talk, and debating and challenging such, on my path to wherever I have ended up.

To my children, Richard, Michael, and Charlotte; for persuading me to overcome, as necessary, my detestation of technological devices and teaching me how to use them, for their considerable contributions to the ideas expounded in this missive, for the lessons they have taught, and are still teaching, me, and for their constant encouragement and support

To my father, Dennis Evans; and this is as much a dedication as an acknowledgement; for being the original, as well as a continuing, inspiration behind whatever I am; your fault as always Dad: for having been a constant sounding board and challenge to my eccentricities; and for always having been a shining example as both a good man and a good citizen.

And last, and very far from least, to my wife, and soulmate, Pamela, without whom this project would not have existed at all; because I may have been the one who produced the actual written manuscript, but in truth it has been a joint project, a path we have been on together, and one we will see out together. She has not only been my guide and stay for most of my adult life, and in many ways my redeemer, but on a more mundane level she has suffered the not inconsiderable inconvenience of having to work to provide the wherewithal for survival whilst I enjoyed the luxury of pursuing a dream.

The Revelation of the Spirit

Chapter One

1: At a time unknown, and in a place that could be anywhere, or everywhere, the Spirit of God was re-manifest and walked amongst humankind, and talked to men and women.

2: She came as a vision, and to the many as well as the few.

3: And the people asked the Spirit who She was;

4: And the Spirit replied: I am that which animates the Word of God; the Creation, the Cosmos.

5: I am the Breath of God.

6: I am the Angel of Light, and the Source of Enlightenment; I am Wisdom.

7: And the people asked the Spirit if She had a name;

8: And the Spirit replied: my name means little: I Am Who I Am; I am Sophia Wisdom; I am Lucifer, the Morning Star, the Angel of Light; I am Ruach, the Breath of God; I am Kali-Ma and Isis and Astarte and Gaia and Freya and Metatron and Parvati, the Essence of both Goddess and God; I Am Who I Am.

9: I am the Creator and the Destroyer, and the path to the Eternal.

10: I am the One who is incarnate in the prophets: Zoroaster, Miriam and Moses, Gautama, Lao-Tse and Confucius, Krishna, Pallas Athene, Socrates, Jesus ben Joseph and Mary of Magdala, Nanak, Baha'Ullah, Kahlil Gibran, and Krishnamurti.

11: And the people asked the Spirit to give them wisdom and grant them enlightenment.

Chapter Two

1: And the people said to the Spirit; speak to us of evil, and whereby we are drawn to it.

2: And the Spirit replied: Evil only exists in your minds; it is something that is internal to all of you: it is not something that exists independently or absolutely, apart and separate from existence.

3: All people have it within them to do good or to do evil. You are complex beings, and it is your nature to be both selfish and altruistic at different points of your existence: none of you can ever be wholly altruistic all the time, or wholly selfish.

4: In the same way that you cannot be good or do good all the time, then in the same way you cannot constantly be evil or do evil.

5: You are capable of doing much good and little evil, or vice-versa, half and half or any other proportion, and over the whole of your life you can do great evil and be a curse on the face of the world, or you can contribute much to the welfare of others.

6: You know with few exceptions the difference between right and wrong: you have had it explained to you on numerous occasions by your prophets and bodhisattvas and messiahs and gurus: so it all comes down to the choices you make.

7: You use your employer's time to conduct your own personal business; is that not stealing, and do you not know that stealing is wrong? You cheat on your partner with your neighbour's partner: do you not know that too is wrong? You spread malicious gossip: is that not wrong?

8: And do you not understand that the one you damage most is yourself?

9: But it is of course always your choice.

10: But these are only what you would consider little evils. Surely you would say they do not compare with the wars, and crusades, and pogroms and concentration camps, and atrocities and holocausts, and acts designed to terrorise? And surely they cannot be placed in the same category as random, mindless, gratuitous acts of extreme violence, or cold blooded tortures inflicted by deranged inquisitions?

11: But, with one exception, they can.

12: Most of these evils are committed by ordinary people, who commit them under the influence of peer pressure, or narcotics, or group dynamics: 'I was only obeying orders': the excuse of the mindless and the cowardly throughout the ages.

13: And then you cause evils to happen by what you think is by mischance or accident, but in truth these too are usually consequent upon choices you made, even if they are actually defaults that occurred because you did not do something you should have done: the brakes on the vehicle that you had been meaning to have fixed, the boiler which you had deferred servicing, or the bill you forgot to settle.

14: And then there are the decisions you make, apparently insignificant at the time, which initiate a chain of events that end in serious inconvenience, disaster or tragedy: the one drink too many that started the fight and ended in hospital; the office flirting that got out of hand and ended in emotional trauma for you and your partners: the tired, overworked medic who struggles on and ends up administering a drug overdose which results in a crippled patient.

15: You did not mean to cause those occurrences; you did not intend those results: you were just lazy, or thought you could not afford to pay, or were too tired; you just did not think at all.

16: But the differences between whether you actually chose to do something, or allowed something to happen because you failed to make a choice, or deferred making a choice, may be of legal import in terms of intent, but are of no consequence in the realm of the spirit because you are ultimately responsible in all cases.

17: And the things you class as great evils, 'pure evil' as you will; your concentration camps and pogroms and holocausts and wars only differ from the little evils in scale and degree, and because they are the result of your collective choices rather than individual ones.

18: They are all evils though and all caused by choices you have made.

19: There is one peculiar exception to this general position though: the individuals that you call psychopaths: people whose minds are so constructed that they are incapable of understanding the difference between right and wrong.

20: They are not people as you usually understand the term: they may be members of the species of animal that has presumptively designated itself homo-sapiens, and they may be sentient, self-aware, but it is the knowledge of good and evil that differentiates you from most other animals and what makes you truly human.

21: In terms of the Spirit psychopaths are dead souls and soul-eaters: their actions may appear from the outside to be pure evil, particularly when they indulge in acts of appalling violence for no reason other than their personal gratification, and their actions may be evils, but in truth they themselves are no more evil than the rock that falls on your head.

22: Psychopaths are just things, they just are; so protect yourself from them, and deal with them as you see fit, but they have nothing to do with evil.

23: In the same way natural disasters are not evil either; they may cause untold suffering but there is no intent; the volcano does not have any desire to kill humans, or anything else for that matter.

24: Only sentient beings that know the difference between right and wrong can commit evil acts, or be regarded in any way as evil; the wasp that stings you is not evil, it is just a wasp.

25: And there is no separate evil entity out there somewhere corrupting humans and forcing them to do things: there never was a Devil other than in the rabid imaginings of deluded priests, or as a construct of devious autocrats who invented one as a means to keep the people in the grip of fear.

26: And then there are things you think are evils but are not: death and poverty and pain.

27: You may call these evil and afflictions, but they are not so in themselves; it is only your imagination that gives them those qualities, and it is within you to change that.

28: And if you can choose, if you are not in some way coerced, then why are you so foolish as to persist in a course which causes you pain; giving sickness, want, and death the status you do, and fearing them as you do?

29: If the essence of these things you fear was able to find a home in you through and by its own authority and volition, as an external entity separate from you, it would dwell alike and the same in all; for you are all of one species, and are provided, in principle and to whatever extent, with the same tools and instruments to judge and understand.

30: But it does not so do, and the diversity of opinions you entertain on these matters clearly shows that they only have their hold over you with your consent; one person perhaps understands their true essence, but a thousand others harbour them in contrary and entirely arbitrary forms.

31: You presume that death, poverty, and pain are your principle enemies.

32: But this death, which too many of you deem 'of all things dreadful the most dreadful'; is in truth, for the few who know and understand it for what it is, a haven from the tempests of your physical existence, nature's finest benefit, and a universal remedy for all ills.

33: It was and is the creation of death that allowed and allows life to change and evolve and grow in understanding: without death life is not life but mere existence.

34: Many of you await her in 'fear and trembling', and yet others can face her more easily than they do all the travails of life.

35: In truth it is not death that is to be feared but the pain that is associated with it, the dying, and its anticipation.

36: And the same can be said for poverty: it is not so much the poverty itself that offends, but the ills associated with it; hunger and thirst, cold and disease; and these too are pain.

37: And pain may be something that you suffer but it is not an evil.

Chapter Three

1: And the people said to the Spirit; speak to us then of suffering. Why do people suffer? And why do the good suffer as much and sometimes more than the bad?

2: And the Spirit replied: suffering is an intrinsic part of existence; it is part and parcel of the material world.

3: The material world is built around change, and so therefore are you.

4: You suffer from what appears to you to be the caprice of nature; from earthquake, fire and flood and tempest, disease and decay; but these are necessary parts of the fabric of existence. Without them there would be no change and there would be no possibility of learning and growing and increasing in understanding.

5: The earthquake and volcano and tempest renew the earth. The volcano fertilises the soil that you use to grow your olives and vines, and it is you who choose to live in its shadow; you reap the benefits it bestows, and in turn you accept the risk that it may in time destroy some of you.

6: The river floods and renews the soil in a similar way, but again it will sometimes flood to excess and destroy your works. As my greatest avatar once put it you would be best advised not to build your houses on the sand.

7: Most of the suffering laid at the door of nature is, in truth, down to choices made by you. Climb the mountain in a snowstorm and you risk freezing to death.

8: And just so disease and decay are necessary:

9: Your bodies contain myriads of microbes which in just one area, for example, enable you to digest your food and excrete waste products, and without them you would be unable to exist; and in the same way your higher functions are totally dependent upon the continued operation of more basic organs.

10: Your brain can think as much as it likes, but if the heart stops pumping blood round your system your brain will soon cease thinking for lack of oxygen.

11: The microbes live and blossom and then perish to the march of their own drum and so do you and your parts.

12: The outer layer of your skin sheds itself daily, and the parts that fall off are dead, but you continue: and on a different time-scale so it is with you: disease and decay are just so vital parts of life: as parts of you are recycled so is the whole.

13: An old hymn of yours is a favourite of mine; beautiful music; but the theology is regrettably false: in some ways, I would it were not, for life would be more peaceable, but it is nevertheless so: 'change and decay in all around I see, oh Thou who changest not, abide with me': this is a misapprehension of God, both as the separating of God from Creation, and in presuming that God, any more than the Cosmos, is unchanging.

14: It is that concept, that understanding, and misunderstanding of God, that lies at the heart of your problem with suffering: 'why does God allow such and such to happen?'

15: If God wished to suspend the laws of gravity and caused the tile falling from the roof to float down and land on your head as a feather, then it would be at least possible for you not to suffer physical pains.

16: If you could not suffer, however, you would not be human as you understand it; you cannot know pleasure without its opposite, and without both you cannot grow in understanding.

17: It can, of course, be even more basic than that: lepers do not feel pain; it is only their sense of smell that tells them they have gangrene, or are on fire. None of you, I think, would choose leprosy over the sensation of physical pain.

18: Even if the laws of physics were suspended, that would not deal with emotional pain; but again few of you would choose to be rid of the sufferings associated with loss or rejection if it meant you had to give up the joys of loving and being loved: without both, and they are the two sides of the same coin, you would be reduced to golems and zombies, soulless automata.

19: And then there are the sufferings that can clearly be laid at the door of humankind; and those are invariably down to choices made by you, either in full consciousness and in the present, or as a consequence of choices made by you or others in the past.

20: Suffering you impose on yourself or others as a result of your current choices is clearly your fault, and you cannot blame God, sundry devils, or anyone else. 'He made me do it' is not good enough. You are responsible for your own choices.

21: The unconscious choices do allow you an element of excuse.

22: Some of you know no better because you are too soaked in your cultural traditions, be they family, tribal, political, cultural or religious, and much of the suffering that appears to descend, unwarranted, on your heads, is in fact a direct consequence of the political and religious systems that you, or your ancestors, have constructed.

23: If you now know that those systems are flawed you can change them, and, if you choose not to do so, you have no grounds for complaint.

24: You will still complain, no doubt, that suffering is somewhat indiscriminate: it seems to target the good as much as the bad.

25: This seems even more unacceptable when it is those who are clearly innocent who suffer: the young mother whose much wanted baby is stillborn, the old lady mugged for her meagre supper, the children born with spina-bifida or cystic fibrosis, the parent whose child is run over by a drunk driver, the wife who has to watch her beloved partner of many years succumb to dementia, the man whose aged body has deteriorated to the point where he has to suffer the indignity of being cared for as an infant, the athlete reduced to quadriplegia by a fall or a mistimed tackle, the passer-by crippled and mutilated by a roadside bomb.

26: Worst of all in some ways are children afflicted with medical disabilities because of the habits of one of their parents: the sins of the parents are not supposed to be visited on their children.

27: The rest of humanity may sympathise and even empathise with you but that is little consolation; it is you and not they who are suffering: it is you whose hopes and dreams may have been shattered.

28: It may be that the capacity to empathise with the suffering of others helps the empathiser to grow in knowledge of the spirit, but that is not much compensation to the one who is suffering.

29: The conventional answers are platitudes and not good enough, you say, and you are right: if the priests tell you it is in some way all part of God's great plan, and you will understand in God's good time, then God is sadistic and malicious, an offensive old coot not worth having as a God, and his priests are idiots;

30: If it is something you need to experience to enable you to grow in this incarnation, then you are requiring the Universal Consciousness to be a masochistic entity, which is nonsense: you cannot grow in understanding if you are born brain-damaged, blind, and deaf, you cannot learn anything through becoming demented, and as a psychopath you are nothing;

31: If it is karmic recompense for offenses you committed in a previous incarnation, which is not much consolation, but nevertheless a better explanation than most, the suffering imposed on you should be related to your offence, and that is clearly not always the case: if you were a drunk driver who caused death or injury in a previous existence then you could be punished, or punish yourself, in this existence, by being reincarnated as a victim of a drunk driver; but what could you possibly have done to merit ending up with a demented partner?

32: It could be that a handicap is not actually karmic, but simply a condition that a soul has decided to take on to allow others to learn through caring for it; the poor and unfortunate might well be unacknowledged saints.

33: But no-one could possibly have done something in a previous life that could warrant their being reborn as a dead soul.

34: The heart of your problem is your presumption that God is good in your understanding of the word, and that is not the case: God and Nature and Existence are one and the same and They are good in the sense of being heart-breakingly beautiful, glorious, majestic, full of wonder and awe-full, and not in the sense of being kind and gentle.

35: The problem is compounded because you are trying to use the human tool of language to describe something that encompasses so much more than language can convey: it can be encapsulated in the personal pronoun used to describe God: if He and She are unacceptable because of their biological associations, and They implies a multitude of gods, you are left with It which is impersonal and therefore sounds insulting.

36: We have therefore to return to the use of the word good to describe God, for just as the word itself can have layers of meaning so God as All-That-Is is comprehensible on a number of different levels.

37: In the sense that God is synonymous with Nature the problem of suffering becomes clearer: Nature is clearly good in one understanding of the word, in that she, he, it, whatever, provides you with all you need in abundance; but equally clearly is not good in the sense of being kind: you only have to consider parasitic wasps that eat their hosts alive from the inside out whilst taking care to consume the vital organs last, and then, if you will, throw into the pot the guinea worms, the cholera bacteria and rabid dogs.

38: There is, unfortunately, no explanation for, or reason behind, much suffering, much as you would there was;

there is no intent; things are just the way they are: and we are left with the fundamental principle that suffering is the essential partner to pleasure, as with love and hate, and good and evil.

39: If God was good in the sense you would like Him or Her to be, there would have to be an evil God of equal power to compensate.

40: We are back where we started: what makes you human is the ability to discriminate between good and evil; and that means, despite the pain it causes you, you have to be able to suffer as well as feel pleasure and joy.

41: Life as you know it is full of problems, illness, aging, accident, and whatever else you see, be they major or minor, and the pain of dealing with those problems is a kind of existential suffering.

42: Your instincts are always, if at all possible, to avoid such pain, be it physical or emotional, and if you cannot avoid it, to banish it as quickly as you can.

43: But much of this pain, particularly the emotional variant, is merely a conflict and a confusion between your will, and what you would will, and reality, and you too often respond by attempting to alter reality to a new version: the breakdown of a relationship was the other person's fault and was nothing to do with you.

44: You are then deceiving yourself, and have started to acquire a neurosis, which is self-defeating because you then pile more layers of self-deceit on top of the original, and end by causing yourself even more suffering.

45: You can learn from existential suffering, but the pain you suffer through having neuroses teaches you nothing.

46: Suffering may be undesirable and not good, but it is not wholly bad for it makes you compassionate, because your own suffering makes you understand and empathise with the suffering of others.

47: And goodness, in the sense of kindness, only develops in response to suffering and need.

48: Tragedies and disasters often bring out the best in you; it is then that you show your love for others, and there is therefore some good in the bad.

49: And it is that experience of love that most opens you to the Universal Consciousness.

Chapter Four

1: And the people said to the Spirit; speak then to us of our religious systems; that we may understand what is wrong with them.

2: And the Spirit replied: your political and religious systems are flawed because they have, at their core, beliefs that can only be considered delusions:

3: Those beliefs attempt to consider God as He, or less often She. God is not limited by or describable in terms of mammalian biology.

4: The Ancient of Days is a stunningly beautiful example of humanity's artistic creativity, and that creativity and ability to conjure visions is part of your God-given capacity to grow in understanding; but to regard that vision as in any sense a realistic conception of God as a discrete entity is living in fantasy land.

5: When you were children you thought as children but you are now adults and it is time to think as adults and give up childish notions.

6: Your beliefs also assume far too often that human beings are the apogee or pinnacle of God's Creation, yet only anthropomorphic arrogance would presume so.

7: Creation is beyond limit and timeless, and to believe that a being as insignificant as man, existing for the insignificant period of time that man has, on a planet as insignificant as Earth, orbiting a not particularly interesting star, in a system on the edge of one galaxy of stars among a multitude of such, is more important to God than all the rest of Creation, is only a perfect example of the only true sin; Stupidity.

8: The belief that God created human beings with an inherent moral flaw, yet requires them to be morally perfect, and then punishes them for failing, is positively lunatic. If it were possible to have grades of perfection then that would be an even more perfect example of sin than believing man to be the pinnacle of God's creation: believing in a stupid God.

9: The belief that Creation is mechanistic and set on a determined path is also nonsense: God becomes responsible for all events, good or ill, and supposedly sentient beings cannot be held accountable for their actions: sentience and free will become illusions and Creation would cease to have a point; God would have created something both useless and worthless.

10: Believing that God wants, never mind needs, to be worshipped; by anyone, or anything, any part of Creation, is another dogma that cannot withstand analysis: the Creator of the universe does not need anything.

11: Needing or wanting praise is an all too human trait, but the sensible ones amongst you do not have a particularly high regard for those who seek or revel in the adulation of the masses; prima donnas and egoists as they are: so why should you think the Goddess, the Lord of All, the Fount and Sustainer of the Cosmos and Existence itself, insofar as He or She can be considered as a discrete entity, rather than the Cosmic Consciousness, should be desirous of praise. You are making God out to be vain.

12: The purpose of prayer is not adulation, or repentance, or supplication, but thanks.

13: Believing that human beings were given dominion over the Earth, to do with it as they please is another piece of defective thinking.

14: Human beings may have acquired the power to do so, but they use that power at their own peril: the physical laws of cause and effect are as powerful as the moral laws; abuse and destruction of the earth's resources will return to haunt humanity.

15: Even thinking that you are in some sense stewards of the earth is arrogant and offensive: you are part of the earth, not separate from her.

16: Then there is the misapprehension that one gender of humanity has authority over another gender. To believe so is ridiculous. You are symbiotes: you cannot survive without each other, and are equal not only in the sight of God, but in all the spheres of existence.

17: The idea that God has placed any human in authority over others, be they king, pope, ayatollah, president, fuhrer, or whatever, is yet another of your delusions. You may elect or select, or just accept and submit to individuals, but that is your choice: God has nothing to do with it.

18: Human religious systems, and the political systems based on them, are not the responsibility of God; there never was a divine right of kings; or a gift of papal infallibility: those who believed they were the beneficiaries of such managed, and still manage, to be both lunatic and megalomaniac at one and the same time, and those who followed them and continue so to do, were and still are idiots.

19: If we move back to the religious core that underlies your political systems you then have the remarkable idea whereby you claim that man was created in the image of God; which leads to the inversion whereby God acquires by association the attributes of man: in effect you have remade God in the image of man: yet another nonsense to add to your collection.

20: Then you have concocted practices that can only be described as abominations: that one human being can own another; a person somehow becomes property; that is an abomination:

21: That people can be locked into a caste system that determines their spiritual status for the whole of their life on earth, without possibility of change, and as a consequence someone can become ritually unclean through contact with another person; that also is an abomination:

22: That God could possibly have ordained punishments which involve mutilation of offenders; another abomination still:

23: That God ordains the practice of mutilating female genitalia to prevent the enjoyment of sexual intercourse; that also is an abomination. The perpetrators of such acts are moral eunuchs and retards and will probably deservedly reincarnate themselves as ugly, frustrated, lonely, schizoid manic depressives in karmic recompense.

24: You might remonstrate that these practices, and others such as parentally determined forced marriages, or regarding a marriage outside one's own caste as somehow dishonourable to your family, are time-hallowed cultural traditions; but there is no excuse for continuing with stupid habits just because they are old.

25: Then you have the daft idea that God considers celibacy to be morally superior to sexual partnership. The matter is simply a personal choice; believing otherwise again makes God stupid. If you all followed that one the human race would die out!

26: Then you have decided that God communicates with people using only 'sacred' languages; Hebrew, Latin, Arabic, or worst of all the gibberish of 'speaking in tongues'. Such a doctrine is a confidence trick perpetrated upon the people by priests and nothing more than a mechanism for retaining social control; it has nothing to do with God.

27: If God has a language that is unchangeable, something that is actually bound to existence, then the only ones you have that fit the bill are mathematics and music.

28: Next you assume that God is pleased when humans wear, or even actually requires them to wear, particular items of apparel, anywhere or at any time: most especially clerical robes, which are nothing more than archaic ceremonial ostentations; and sacks or bags ordered to cover your females so that seeing them does not excite your males.

29: Those who perpetrate this nonsense are using an utterly defective vision of God; which, if they actually believe it, makes them certifiable lunatics; and if they do not, makes them frauds and charlatans who have designed such solely to inflate their own sense of self-importance, so they can lord it over their neighbours.

30: Then you seek or claim Divine support for your human superstition. Cows and monkeys are not 'sacred', pigs and dogs are not unclean, male circumcision may be a medical issue but it has nothing to do with religion, women do not need to seek 'purification' after oestrus, and cadavers can be disposed of howsoever it pleases the relatives and authorities.

31: Then you have cooked up the wonderful claim that God is interested in ceremony. A God who cares about the order in which candles are lit or the colour of altar cloths is not so much stupid as ridiculous.

32: Last but far from least you seem to think that God is pleased by vastly excessive expenditure of time, effort and resources on constructing and decorating buildings for the celebration or worship of the divine.

33: Quite the contrary of course: the gold plated temples belong to Mammon: they should be scrapped and the monies given back to the poor who were conned into donating them in the first place.

34: If you wish to be connected to the Divine Essence, to the Lord God, Herself and Himself, then sweep away this mould and start anew.

35: Some of you have already begun:

36: Too many of you have belief systems, be they religious or secular, agnostic or atheistic, which are superficial and simplistic; such are hardly thinking at all;

37: Many more of you have institutionalised beliefs which conform to your established religions; legalistic systems with a fossilised mode of thought, which might, just, constitute an improvement on no thought;

38: Some of you have developed a more individualistic way of seeing your world; such are those who believe in the doctrines of the scientific mind-set: reason, scepticism, humane and liberal views on morality; and those are at least using their cerebral cortexes;

39: Such people may think of themselves as having moved beyond religion itself; they are of the opinion that they have no need for outdated sentiments, cultural baggage and traditions that are irrational;

40: In truth though they are closer to the spiritual core of existence than those locked in the grip of old time religion; simply because of their humanity and liberalism;

41: Those of you who are closest to the truth, however, are the few who realise that the rational view, though still necessary, is not on its own sufficient;

42: Such are the ones who retain their love of the rational, but also instinctively know that there is something more;

43: They are the ones who are reaching for the sacrament at the core of existence, the beauty of holiness.

Chapter Five

1: And the people said to the Spirit; speak to us of property and possessions. We place much value in them. Are we deluded?

2: No, you are not deluded:

3: You need your food and clothes and homes and means of transport, and they are therefore of value to you; so value them, care for them and look after them; just make sure that you own them and they do not own you.

4: You need these things, but you do not need an excess of them: enough should be sufficient.

5: There is nothing wrong with having a nice home, but you do not need several, and you do not need mansions or palaces; having such is taking far more than your fair share; and those who do own such are quite simply being greedy.

6: There is nothing wrong with having nice clothes, particularly the ones you wear for parties and celebrations; but again having a wardrobe full is excessive and wasteful of the limited resources of your world.

7: Wearing outfits only one or two times before disposing of them, or buying new ones simply to keep up with fickle fashion, is even worse.

8: Wear and enjoy jewellery if you wish, but pick the items that are simple and elegant and inexpensive rather than those that are expensive and ostentatious; if you have the latter you will only end up worrying about security and theft.

9: By all means have a nice automobile, but you do not need several, and you do not need limousines that cost a fortune, monstrosities that guzzle fuel, or ego-massaging turbo-charged sports machines designed to be driven at dangerous speeds.

10: You can only live in one house at a time, drive in one car at a time, ride one camel at a time, wear one set of clothes at a time.

11: So why do think you need to own all these things; is it just to show off and advertise your wealth?

12: And as for food, eat well and partake of the bounty of the earth, but lay off the over-priced and over-rated gourmet delicacies: fish eggs and snails are for when you are starving and cannot afford anything better: start with the beef steak or nut cutlets, move on to the burgers, and leave the rubbish to last resort.

13: Foie-gras and battery farming are abominations; what have the geese and ducks and chickens done to deserve that?

14: Treat your farm animals as you would wish to be treated: allow them some enjoyment of life, even if that means you have to eat less meat, and when you kill them for food remember to thank them, for in their dying they have given you the means to live.

15: Then of course you have your money, and that is only a means of exchange; pieces of metal and bits of paper; and once again something you need, but yet again in the quantity of enough is sufficient.

16: The love of money is not the root of all evil, but love of money for its own sake is certainly an evil; it rots the soul; the miser is already in hell.

17: And all of this is mere frippery. You cannot take any of it with you when you go.

18: As Jesus ben Joseph said; "Store not up treasures here on earth, where moths and rust will destroy them, and thieves break in and steal them."

19: If you want your place in paradise assured, then the best adage is that of the Society of Friends; live simply that others may simply live.

20: Beware of titles and honours! Those earned honestly, and which describe an honourable profession, are deserved and can be worn with pride, provided only that such pride is not unseemly; medics and academics have truly earned their appellations.

21: Archaic titles and ostentations and modes of address, however, are worthless fripperies; they serve no purpose other than the massaging of personal egos at the supposed expense of those foolish enough to be impressed by such.

22: The religious ones are probably the most offensive; if the bearers of them actually understood their own theologies they would surely realise that the titles they hold and the way they allow their followers to address them is, in terms of that theology idolatrous and probably blasphemous.

23: The fact that their theologies are rubbish is irrelevant; they should at least have the decency to practise what they preach.

24: Supreme pontiff, reverend father, your holiness, grand mufti, grand ayatollah, your eminence; whatever: these are all titles abrogated to themselves by pompous imbeciles and swallowed wholesale by ignorant grovelling peons.

25: The monarchical and aristocratic equivalents are less hypocritical but no more justified: God has no interest in seeing you grovel before Her, so why on earth, or anywhere else for that matter, can you see anything worthwhile in bowing and scraping to other human beings?

26: Your leaders, and those who aspire to be leaders, do not need pompous titles; they need to remember that their function is to serve their people, not lord it over them.

27: Kings and queens, emperors and empresses, maharajas and maharanis, sultans and sultanas; call them what you will; all this does nothing but inflate their own sense of self-importance. Aristocrats have even less justification for their assumption of power and privilege: they hold both without necessary responsibility; the prerogative of you know whom throughout history.

28: Hereditary titles are the biggest nonsense of all: someone holds a dukedom, and is called duke, which is derived from the Latin dux, meaning general, because some ancient ancestor was granted it in perpetuity by some deranged monarch whose commode he had emptied.

29: Have a purge and clear out the junk, and while you are at it, get rid of relics from long lost and not regretted imperial pasts; what is the point in the Order of some long lost Empire, or the Order of the Suspender belt?

Try the order of the flying pig instead; it would probably be more appropriate.

30: Medals should be for soldiers, awarded for bravery above and beyond the call of duty, and honours, if you would have them, they should be for exceptional, voluntary, service to the community, not for simply doing what you have been paid for, and they should never be inherited by your heirs.

31: There are, of course, other forms of possession that are truly valuable; your experiences, memories and associations; these are worth so much more than things.

32: Children and families and colleagues and friends should be cherished far above and beyond material possessions: in truth, apart from yourself, your memories of them are all you take with you when you leave this frame of existence.

33: Just remember that you do not own them, and most particularly you do not own your children; they are gifts from God; they have their own lives to live and paths to follow; help and encourage them where you can; but do not try to live your lives vicariously through them; any successes or failures they may have are theirs and theirs alone, not yours.

Chapter Six

1: And the people said to the Spirit; speak to us of our souls. What are they? And speak to us of death. What happens when our life here is over?

2: And the Spirit replied: you do not have a soul, you are a soul.

3: You think of yourselves as physical matter animated by a soul or by the spirit, but this is an illusion: physical matter is but one form of energy and the spirit is also a form of the same energy.

4: God is in some ways a discrete entity; the Fount and Sustainer of the Cosmos, All That Is Not; but in other ways God is the Cosmos, All-That-Is: God is the energy that flows through everything and makes Existence itself conscious.

5: You are part of that Consciousness, and therefore part of God: you are daughters and sons of God, children of God.

6: God is everything, and every part of everything, so you too are in a very real sense God.

7: When your physical body completes its current incarnation; dies, to use the common parlance, then it is broken up into its constituent elements and is recycled to something new: dust to dust, ashes to ashes and worms shall eat you up.

8: The constituent energy remains though: it has only reformed.

9: This has been going on since, in the time that is part of your physical existence, the dawn of the universe: the elements that make up your physical bodies were constructed in the stars, and from the death-throes of exploding super-novae; you are truly born of the stars, you are Star-dust.

10: And the earth to which your physical body returns on death, will itself one day be swallowed up by the dying Sun, and the whole will dissipate across the Cosmos, to be recycled to new star systems.

11: In the same way, on your death, your consciousness returns to whence it came; the Universal Consciousness, the energy that permeates existence.

12: You no longer sense yourself as a totally independent entity, for the illusion of the passage of time has gone; left behind in the physical world to which it is inextricably tied.

13: For the Consciousness you return to when you die, God, Eternity, is timeless; the idea of time passing means nothing to It; God does not wake up in the morning and think, what shall I do today?

14: But the fabric of the Universe itself is timeless so why should you expect anything different for the Being that created the Universe and is the Universe?

15: Things that are subject to time grow and age and die. The energy that constitutes the Universe does not register time; photons do not age, they just are.

16: Energy is conserved: it changes form, but is neither created anew nor destroyed.

17: Time is intimately linked to space; together they make up space-time. They can no more be separated than good can be separated from evil, and light can be separated from dark.

18: When you are separated and disconnected from space, you are automatically separated and disconnected from time.

19: In this world you are a physical body, a thing; but this is only what you appear to be, something that is in perpetual motion, constantly changing, and varyingly conscious of that change.

20: You are, as it were, a hologram; a part that contains the whole, but is clearly also distinguishable from the whole.

21: The same can be said for all matter: all particles too are a part of the whole but at the same time contain the whole.

22: If we were able to take a human being and squash all the empty space out of them, we would be left with a miniscule portion of solid substance smaller than the eye could see.

23: You are creatures made up largely of nothing; your insubstantial bodies are tiny constructs of solid matter held together by electromagnetic, nuclear, and gravitational forces; the conventional form of matter that you think you are, but which is just an illusion.

24: But in truth you are not a thing, you are consciousness, awareness, both changing and unchanging.

25: Your physical body is but a part of the flow of consciousness that you experience.

26: The physical world is an illusion, a dream dreamt by the Universal Consciousness;

27: You and I and God are each others' dream.

28: Reincarnation is usually thought of as being re-born into this world, returning here, but this world only exists as an extension of consciousness.

29: The physical world is not something you can enter and leave: it is an unfolding of the illusion within consciousness.

30: And the illusion is not limited to the experience of this existence, vast and wonderful as it is; for in totality, the illusion is an infinity of imagined existences, of which your existence is but one.

31: When the illusion of appearing to be a person in this existence ends, it is replaced by another dimension of the imagination which will not necessarily bear any resemblance to the illusion you are currently participating in.

Chapter Seven

1: And the people said to the Spirit; speak to us of salvation. What must we do to reach paradise? What is paradise? And is there a hell?

2: And the Spirit replied: there is no salvation, because there is nothing you need to be saved from other than things you can save yourself from.

3: As Jesus said; "Physician, heal yourself."

4: Fear itself is the only thing you need to be afraid of, and resolving that, which is within your own power, is the only sensible meaning of salvation.

5: Paradise or heaven, and for that matter hell, are not places in some non-existent hereafter; somewhere you are sent after death; a reward or punishment for being good or bad boys and girls during your sojourn as physical entities.

6: Heaven and hell are both states of being.

7: Heaven and hell are both here on Earth, in this present existence, and in all other physical realms; here in your minds you create your own heaven and hell; if you are happy, enjoying yourselves, you are in heaven; if you are miserable you are in hell.

8: Your experience of the physical world can be hellish or heavenly; hellish if you are trapped in the illusion of separate identity, and addicted to your egoistic desires; heavenly if you are aware of your essential unity with the rest of creation.

9: Your life in the physical world is always important.

10: Just understand that life is good and there is nothing to fear in death.

11: All the sensory events, feelings and emotions you experience in this life can be accepted, enjoyed, or enthused over.

12: There are tasks you have to do in your daily life; practical or social, work or leisure related, major or minor; deadlines to meet, appointments to keep, drudgeries and challenges:

13: Enthuse whenever you can, and if you cannot manage to be enthusiastic, enjoy as much as you can; pleasure can be had from the most mundane of tasks if you have the right attitude.

14: Where you find you cannot be enthusiastic or full of joy when contemplating a task, and it would take someone exceptional to be enthusiastic or joyful when faced with a blocked drain, or a boil that needs lancing, then accept it and get on with it; it still needs to be done; will not disappear if you ignore it; and will probably leave you feeling satisfied or at least relieved on completion.

15: If you find yourself in a circumstance, be it tied to a task, or a relationship, personal or employment, which you find intolerable then change it or leave it.

16: If you are unsure of which way to go, if you are confused by the trials and tribulations of the daily round; then a good guide to whether you have made a decision that is correct for you at a given moment is if you sense relief:

17: It feels as if you have been swimming upstream against the current and have now turned about and are swimming with the flow.

18: There is of course the obverse, in the dualism which rules existence: whereby the broad path which is the common path of your world is too often the wrong one, and the narrow path of the few is the correct one.

19: Remember what Jesus said; "forbid not little children to come unto me; for of such is the kingdom of God."

20: Children know pain as much as adults, but they are able to empathise with the pain of others more instinctively than adults; they are capable of responding in just the right way at just the right time; they know what to do without knowing why; and they somehow banish the pain and wipe away the tears.

21: The smile of a child lights up the world.

22: We know of course that they can also be cruel and thoughtless, but that is again just instinctive.

23: What they have that is special in terms of salvation, however, is their boundless capacity for joy and fun; their ability to enthuse; they have the keys to paradise; for they have not yet discovered the pleasures of world-weariness or cynicism.

24: That is not to say that you are expected to revert to being little children: that is neither practical nor possible; you are adults, with the tasks and responsibilities of adults, and you cannot evade those obligations.

25: What you need to relearn from the children is having the right attitude.

26: Follow your best instincts and you will not go far wrong.

27: If you are enjoying most of what you do, enthusing about some of what you do, and are able to accept the rest with equanimity, then you have found heaven on earth.

28: And you, by your attitude, put yourself there.

29: If you find much of your circumstance intolerable, and you are miserable, then you have planted yourself in hell. Change things and get out.

30: If you would know more then hearken to the words of Sri Aurobindo; 'Cut yourselves asunder from the snares of the mind and the senses; the traps of the theologians and the priests; the meshes of the scriptures and the bondage of ideas.

31: All of these imprison our spirit; lock it in with forms; so we must go beyond, far beyond; renouncing the lesser for the greater, the finite for the Infinite; proceeding from illumination to illumination, from experience to experience, and from soul-state to soul-state.

32: Hold not even to the truths we hold most dear, for they are but forms and expressions of the Ineffable who refuses to let Itself be limited by any form or expression.'

Chapter Eight

1: And the people said to the Spirit; are there then no moral certainties; is everything relative? Speak to us of sin. What is it?

2: And the Spirit replied: God is not interested in constructing a set of rules and punishing people for disobeying them.

3: There never was a state of innocence in which you existed in some primaeval epoch, and from which you fell.

4: The knowledge of good and evil is an essential part of what makes you human.

5: Therefore there cannot possibly be a need to atone for being human; you can only be required to atone for something which you chose to do.

6: Having to atone for what you are, as opposed to what you have done is a nonsense: should you have to atone for having red hair, being tall or short, or having a different skin colour?

7: The only circumstances in which you could ever be regarded as living in a state of innocence, are when you are very young infants, are in an advanced state of dementia, are in a vegetative state, or in the special conditions that apply to psychopaths and other dead souls, in other words when you are only homo and not homo sapiens.

8: In effect the classic doctrine of atonement as espoused by your established religions is, and always was, rubbish.

9: Sin is separation or alienation from God. We cannot in some ways ever be separated from God because we are part of God and God is all of us.

10: To quote Sri Aurobindo; 'All separateness is an illusion, and all things are ultimately interconnected and whole'.

11: There are those who have chosen to alienate themselves from God, both intellectually and spiritually; your Bin Ladens, Pol Pots, and Stalins; they are the dead souls and already in hell, because they have disconnected themselves from the rest of humanity, and hence from the God that dwells in humanity.

12: They are still part of God in the sense that God is present in a slug, a nettle, sand, and everything else, but alienated from God in the sense of God as Universal Consciousness.

13: The only way you can talk of an era of innocence, some sort of lost 'golden age', without talking nonsense, is by referring back to pre-historical times, for then you knew both more and less than you do now: in some ways you were much wiser than you now are, and at the same time it could be said you were more innocent.

14: According to your oldest belief systems, all life as it is known today, human, mammal, bird, reptile, fish, bug and plant is part of one never changing, inter-connected system, a huge network of relationships which can be traced all the way back to your Spirit Ancestors in the Dreamtime.

15: But your communal consciousness then fractured; and your awareness of that communal consciousness became occluded as it fragmented into your separate egos.

16: You acquired new ideas, thoughts, and concepts; and one of the most fundamental was that you buried your perception of the female aspects of divinity: your god became male and male alone.

17: As your Communal Dreaming faded your ego-self found itself alone and vulnerable, with nothing to support it but your remote and remorseless new god.

18: Your 'fall' from innocence, the Fall, is no more than that fracture in consciousness.

19: You also found yourselves staring at a new and terrible image; the spectre of death.

20: For in the Dreamtime your dead were always with you; still real in the memories of the living, but in your new 'reality' you have banished them from the consciousness; they are part of your memory but no longer thought of as real.

21: You need to hold on to your new understanding, and your new knowledge, but you also need to rediscover the old truths, and bind the two together in a whole that is greater than the sum of the parts.

22: You have only forgotten the Universal Consciousness; it was always there waiting for you to remember.

23: And your 'dead' have not gone; they too are part of the Universal Consciousness in its totality and also as still extant separate entities.

24: You only 'understand' that they are gone because you do not understand the nature of time; that it is an illusion:

25: There are those of you who are conscious of your 'dead' as spirit entities, and are able to contact them to seek their advice, just as you used to when they were 'alive'.

26: Those who claim to use a connection to the dead to tell you what the future holds for you are either delusional or charlatans; because time is an illusion, the future may already be here, 'the days of future passed', and in that sense the future is known, but time in your existence does not work that way, and your future in your world is not knowable to you.

27: As to moral relativism, it is indeed true that there are few moral certainties and even fewer absolutes.

28: Stealing is wrong, but if your family is starving and you have no other means of providing for their immediate needs, then stealing some food, presuming that others around you deny you the charity that the moral laws demand of them, is clearly less of an offence against God than allowing your family to starve would be.

29: The greater moral offence is given by those who, by denying you their charity, leave you no alternative but to steal.

30: The essentials, as always, are to treat others as you would be treated yourself, and to consume all things in moderation.

31: If you wish to insist on using the language of sin, then sin is offence against me, me in you, me in others, you in others, and all of us in God.

32: There are small sins, middle sized sins, and great sins.

33: All sins, however, can be remitted. There is no such thing as an unforgivable sin, though if you do not repent of whatever sin you commit you may not be able to forgive yourself.

34: Small sins are those you commit against yourself, and against your own portion of the Holy Spirit, your share of me.

35: Medium sins are those committed against other beings.

36: And the great sins are those committed against the many.

37: Nothing is absolute though: remember, the guide is always the Golden Mean.

38: The physical body is a temple for me, for the spirit within you. If you abuse or damage it through the use of recreational drugs, or through excessive or insufficient consumption of food, or through exercising too much or not enough, you commit only a minor sin.

39: If the abuse starts to affect others though, then the sin becomes greater, since sins which affect only you can be remedied by ceasing to indulge in the activity, whereas sins which affect others require also restitution, contrition, and apology.

40: What you call sin is in truth a form of obsessive behaviour, and, ultimately, a waste of time.

Chapter Nine

1: And the people said to the Spirit; speak to us of behaviour. What are the moral laws? What should we do? How do we become good people, and how do we become good citizens.

2: And the Spirit replied: you can give or you can take. You can live and grow, you can mark time and stand still, or you can fester and die. The choice as always is yours.

3: Live life for today. The past has gone and tomorrow never comes. Take life as it comes and enjoy what it has to offer.

4: Live life to the full but remember that moderation in all things is also best. The body is built for pleasure but it is also a temple, and an excess of anything does it no good.

5: Live simply so that others may simply live. Live intentionally and with restraint, and live a life true to your core beliefs.

6: Do unto others as you would be done unto. One of the major purposes of life is to help other beings whenever and wherever we can.

7: Never treat others as a mere means to an end.

8: God is in every person, and in all Creation. Try to live in such a way as to remove all occasions and excuses for conflict, whether they be between individuals, families, tribes, nations, or species.

9: Be polite to others whenever possible. Manners may not maketh man but they certainly help oil the wheels of a civilised society.

10: Every single person needs to feel wanted; and also needs to feel able to contribute to society: as a corollary all who can contribute to society, no matter in how small a way, should; and those who can and wilfully do not are not entitled to receive any of the benefits of society. They are on route to perdition if not already there.

11: Live in accordance with our Divine inspiration; recognize both your own gifts and needs, and those of others, and learn to support one another. You then will have a real community, whether it is a family, a school, a neighbourhood, a country, the world, or all that is.

12: Tread lightly on the Earth. Just as you arrive on the Earth with nothing and leave with nothing, and add nothing while you sojourn here, so you should take as little as possible too. If you sustain the Earth She will sustain you: if you are destroyers of life then in the end She will destroy you.

13: Look always for your soulmate. It may take many existences, but if you are fortunate enough to find such you are indeed blessed, for your souls can meld to become as one.

14: For those who are not so fortunate there is much compensation to be had from the friends and companions you find in your wider society.

15: Seek also your home. Be it in this existence or another one there is a special piece of this world also waiting for everyone; somewhere to walk barefoot and feel your feet dance and your heart sing.

16: Know that death is the other side of life, and there is a time for you to leave this existence. Cling not to life when that time arrives, and accept with gladness your transfer to the next level of consciousness.

17: Learn to love yourself for what you are. If you fail to do that then you cannot love others.

18: To live a balanced and spiritually whole life, you need to be truly in harmony with yourself and aligned with your beliefs and values.

19: Be faithful and consistent as you live the truth, and let your life speak.

20: God is in every person. You are beings who are all spiritually equal, but each of you is born to express that divinity in your own special ways.

21: All of life is sacramental; all persons are valuable, and the sacramental life, religion if you would have it, is inseparable from everyday living, so make it so.

22: Make space to contemplate the eternal. The last purpose of life is to reach enlightenment: the knowledge that you are part of the Universal Consciousness; both a child of God, and God Herself and Himself.

Chapter Ten

1: And the people said to the Spirit; speak to us of purpose. Why are we here? What are we for?

2: And the Spirit replied: there is purpose for God and there is purpose for you.

3: For God as Everything That Is; Existence, the Cosmos, the all pervading force that is life, there is no purpose, only experience.

4: Purpose implies a future; the passage of time, and for God as all of these there is no passage of time, only now.

5: And for God as Everything That Is Not; Non-being, the same must apply.

6: For God as Being; Universal Consciousness, the One; then the divine purpose is to see the growth in Creation of sentience and understanding, and the return of all to the One.

7: For creatures that are both material and sentient time appears to exist, and they therefore can have purpose.

8: That purpose is individual and personal. Every man or woman is free, and entitled to find their own path to heaven or hell. Every woman or man shall find their own truth and their own purpose.

9: There is purpose for you in this existence as it is, and purpose in this existence that is connected to the Eternal, to God, the Universal Consciousness, the One.

10: You can have purpose in this existence as it is in many ways: finding a partner and raising and bringing up a family; building a business and supplying goods that fit the needs of others; teaching the young; ministering to the sick and the poor and the elderly; farming the land; mediating disputes; law-making and administering government; soldiering; and many more, and all of these are capable of giving your life meaning, and can, therefore, be good in themselves.

11: To be good in themselves, they only need to be carried out with good intent: seek only to be as unselfish as you can, and do unto others as you would be done unto yourself.

12: And learn to enjoy your life, for that too gives purpose.

13: If you can live for the present and appreciate the goodness around you, rather than see too much of the dark side of life, you will enjoy yourself, and in the process spread that goodness without any apparent effort.

14: Smile and the world smiles with you!

15: To find purpose in this existence that is connected to the Eternal, to God, the Universal Consciousness, the One, involves study and thought and meditation; attention to your inner being.

16: Seek to learn and understand: take heed of the teachings of your prophets and gurus and messiahs and bodhisattvas.

17: Look at what they really had to say about how to live your lives, and follow their instructions, and you will find your lives are both happy and purposeful.

18: Ultimately, though it may take many lifetimes to achieve it, you, and all other sentient beings will at last understand, and make your way home to the One.

19: To paraphrase T. S. Eliot; 'Cease not from exploration, and the end of all your exploring will be to arrive back where you started and know the place for the first time.'

20: It may well be that such understanding, when it does finally arrive, will most commonly arrive with maturity; the thought and contemplation involved need to be given time.

21: A very few exceptional individuals; the prime examples of whom were Jesus ben Joseph and Gautama, may have that vision as young people; and they have the often unenviable task of leading a large portion of humanity through a significant leap to a higher level of understanding.

22: In general though younger beings are in the nature of things more concerned with life in the here and now. And that is as it should be.

23: That life as well is undoubtedly lived best if it too has a purpose, and that is most appropriately framed as do unto others as you would be done unto. This is well if limited to other members of your own species, better still if expanded to include other forms of life, and best of all if it encompasses the Cosmos.

24: As William Blake had it; 'To see a world in a grain of sand, and a heaven in a wild flower, hold infinity in the palm of your hand, and eternity in an hour'.

25: Creatures that are material but not sentient cannot in their present existence have purpose: they just are. In the course of evolution though, their forms may develop sentience and hence purpose, and thereby fulfil the Will of God.

26: Be aware though there is no place such as El Dorado, and no Shangri La; the grass is not greener on the other side.

27: Some seek adventure and excitement, some seek happiness, some seek contentment and peace, but these things are not to be found in one place and not another; they are things that are within you, and you can have them, or not, as the case may be, anywhere.

28: You can live amidst luxury and be surrounded by beauty, and you can possess untold wealth, but not have the things that really matter to you; and you can live amidst poverty and be surrounded by ugliness, and own no material possessions, and yet have all that your inner being desires; all is up to you to choose.

29: You can live free in the most liberal state in the world and be miserable, chained in irons that you, and you alone, put there; and you can live under the most bureaucratic, illiberal, reactionary restrictions imposed by the most tyrannical of regimes, yet be free at heart and content and happy with yourself; the choice is yours.

30: Who you are and what you are is something entirely of your own making. Running after an elusive and in truth illusory paradise is chasing rainbows; you are actually running away from yourself.

31: You will no doubt ask about those who appear to be condemned, through no apparent fault, to live in grinding poverty. How are poor peasants supposed to find purpose amidst their struggle to survive?

32: And what about the infirm old, the sick, and the invalids? Others may find purpose in helping them, but how can they themselves achieve anything? How can they find understanding, or achieve enlightenment, when they have not the resources, time, abilities, or whatever else that is needed?

33: No matter how much life may be a struggle, almost everyone is still able to make a contribution to making this world a better place: there is always room for that smile, and there is always an opportunity to give thanks.

34: Even if the cares of the world seem irredeemably burdensome, they are never so heavy that you cannot spare time to help others.

35: Not everyone can be an Einstein or a Beethoven, never mind a Jesus or a Gautama, but everyone is capable of recognising that there is beauty in existence, and sensing thereby a connection to the Universal Consciousness, to God.

36: In the words of Einstein; 'A human being is part of a whole, called by us the Universe, a part limited in time and space.

37: We experience ourselves, our thoughts and feelings, as something separated from the rest, a kind of optical delusion of our consciousness. This delusion is a prison for us, restricting us to our personal desires and to affection for a few persons nearest to us.

38: Our task must be to free ourselves from this prison by widening our circles of compassion to embrace all living creatures and the whole of nature in all its beauty and glory'.

39: It is also your task to create, or co-create with God if you will, your life, with all its experiences, and possibly your death as well.

40: You are both partaking in and conducting an experiment; and you are an experiment.

Chapter Eleven

1: And the people said to the Spirit; speak to us then of employment. You say we can all find purpose in our daily lives, but surely all activities are not good?

2: And the Spirit replied: Most jobs are good in themselves; but you can have too much of a good thing; an excess of anything turns even the good to evil.

3: An individual person is generally a good, and the arrival of a baby is generally regarded as something to celebrate, but the arrival of a tenth child to parents struggling to feed the nine they already have is at best a mixed blessing, and as we move through the circumstance where there are so many people that you have thousands dying of famine, and eventually to the point where the numbers are so great that the very earth is degraded to the extent that the society itself dies; then the people, individual goods though they may be, have, as a mass, turned into a pestilence, a cancer; and then so it is with employments.

4: On a more mundane level, eating one bar of chocolate is pleasurable; eating two bars of chocolate is more pleasurable, but probably not twice as pleasurable; and eating ten bars of chocolate at one sitting will make you sick.

5: Most jobs are good jobs: farmers, gardeners, miners, fishermen, manufacturers, traders, salesmen, teachers, carers, nurses, doctors, plumbers, electricians, carpenters, refuse collectors, truck drivers and train drivers, sailors, scientists, engineers, policemen, firemen, soldiers; all are needed by your societies;

6: Accountants, lawyers, bankers, stockbrokers, bureaucrats, tax collectors, priests, vintners and brewers, writers, musicians, athletes, thespians and prostitutes also have their place.

7: Even your pet hates: politicians, estate agents, insurance salesmen and journalists, have their uses; they all are necessary to the smooth functioning of your complex society.

8: But careless farming can denature the soil and pollute watercourses, mining and manufacturing use up limited resources and degrade the environment, overfishing destroys stocks; all destroy habitats of other creatures.

9: Manufacturing in addition, alongside its trading adjuncts, sometimes produces things deliberately constructed to incorporate built in obsolescence, so their customers need to purchase replacements in short order. It would be better, and less wasteful, if they were made repairable.

10: Change for the sake of change, driven by so-called fashion, and intended only to generate unnecessary and excessive consumption, is also a waste of resources.

11: Manufacturing, allied to human invention, sometimes also produces undesirable products: vacuum cleaners are a clear benefit to you; they reduce drudgery; but other powered devices can not only be unnecessary but can make you lazy.

12: Jobs that are in the nature of being good in themselves can end up producing bad effects by excess of quantity or by unforeseen consequence: too many public employees ends up creating a level of government debt that is unserviceable.

13: There is no point in paying people to dig holes in roads just to fill them in.

14: In addition some jobs can be good or bad, depending on the attitude of the people doing them; there are good and bad lawyers, bankers, politicians, bureaucrats, etc: those that are good are those where the primary desire is to serve the good of humanity; those that are bad are those that are primarily concerned with self-interest.

15: All of you necessarily have the interests of yourselves and your loved ones at heart; they are hot-wired into your biological system, and no-one can be completely selfless; it is only when your motives and actions are predominantly selfish that there is a problem.

16: A lawyer who uses his oratorical and analytical skills to keep his criminal but rich client out of gaol is abusing his talent; he may be a brilliant lawyer but he is a rotten soul.

17: It goes without saying that some occupations: people making a living as gun runners, drug smugglers, bootleggers, pimps, pirates, burglars, muggers, fraudsters, loan sharks, etc; largely classed as criminals by sensible societies, are out of order: there can be no excuse for such activities; it should be blatantly obvious even to the malefactors themselves that their 'businesses' destroy the lives of others.

18: And then there are the popes, ayatollahs, televangelists, mahdis, dictators and kings, who are not only useless but dangerous.

19: Some activities though, notionally bad in principle, are understandable and should be treated with circumspection: someone who steals food because they are starving, who grows opium poppies or cuts down a patch of tropical forest to grow crops because it is the only way they can provide for their family; such are more of an indictment on a society which allows such circumstances to exist than a condemnation of the notional miscreants.

20: Some employments are useless and unnecessary rather than bad by definition: running betting shops, casinos, short haul airlines; working as bull-fighters, pornographers, arms dealers, mercenaries, speculators, tabloid journalists, paparazzi, sociologists, cosmetic surgeons to the vain, fashion designers; all of whom are irritating and should find something better to do with their lives.

21: And then there are the most useless 'employments' of all: people who make a living out of being famous for the sake of being famous, and who provide the base for your appalling celebrity culture; and effectively create the wallies who waste their lives obsessing over such nonentities.

22: Finally you have created a society where you reward some people with ridiculously excessive levels of remuneration, and underpay others who are more useful and more worthy.

23: There is nothing wrong with people making a living as actors, musicians, professional footballers, and even investment bankers; the former entertain you and brighten your lives, and the latter manage your pension and other funds; but paying some of them as you do creates a society that is fundamentally defective.

24: They do not need that much money; they only blow it on fripperies; sports cars, race horses, gambling, mink coats, diamonds, and champagne; and it then inflates their egos to the extent that they turn into prima donnas.

25: Rearrange things and give the monies to your refuse collectors, farm workers, and carers.

26: You need to have an equitable society for it to be a happy and contented one.

Chapter Twelve

1: And the people said to the Spirit; teach us how to learn; that we may better understand.

2: You all have the facility to learn: you were born to learn: you have been gifted with a brain that is designed for learning.

3: You start learning in your mother's womb, carry on from your birth and continue until the day you die;

4: When you cease learning then you are already dead; your body may still be functioning, but that is all; you are no longer living but only existing.

5: Learn from the natural world, and the people around you as well as from books and from teachers. Look and see and you will find learning comes naturally.

6: Look at the rest of creation; learn from the animal world, the world of the plants, the microscopic realms, the rocks and the stars; they have much to say.

7: As Terence White had it the ants and bees mirror the politics of fascism and communism, and the geese and whales demonstrate the politics of freedom and equality.

8: The trees show forth in all its glory the beauty of community: how many varieties of animal life live in and on an oak?

9: The microscopic world and the stars give you visions of your insignificance; in terms of your tiny part in the grand scheme of things; but at the same time they remind you of your true significance; because although you are all destined to die, you know that is the case, and they do not, which makes you greater than them.

10: Contemplating the butterflies and dragonflies, the mountains and seas and glades, reveals the wonders of Creation, and inspires the dreams of the beauty of holiness and the holiness of beauty; peace and tranquillity abound in their contemplation.

11: Learn the skills of your craft as you must: you need such to earn your living; and there is much joy to be had from a craft well learnt, but leave time for the natural sciences and philosophy; they are the underpinnings of understanding and knowing the Eternal.

12: Learn from your children as well as teach them, and cherish the wisdom that can come with old age: both will return you from the daily grind to the essential core of being.

13: Use your brain: study and learn to think for yourselves.

14: And remember that even if you have a lifetime of accumulated knowledge, and even more presume to wisdom, others, including mayhap your students, will challenge you with new ideas; and it is your charge not only to guide change, but also to be open to it: then you may indeed have wisdom.

15: If you would teach others, then also recognise that people are individuals; they are not born equal and with equal talents, and they should be treated according to their needs rather than according to some ridiculous notion of equality.

16: Just remember that those who presume to teach others take on the finest task that is given to any being, and the most rewarding task as well, but also the most demanding and challenging: get it wrong and you mess up the future of those others.

17: And at some point you are all teachers; consider only the vixen who teaches her cubs to hunt and avoid traps, you too teach your own children.

18: I am with Milton on the idiocy of trying to make poets out of ignorant young boys; 'forcing the empty wits of children to compose theme, verses, and orations': poetry is the product of mature thought or rare talent.

19: Mozart at five may have composed symphonies, but give most children of that age an instrument and they only make a noise.

20: So do not force Shakespeare down the throats of those who are functionally illiterate!

21: The objective of education is not simply to teach grammar and mechanics, but to inflame students with the love of learning, and that means apprising and seizing their interest.

22: The other main thrust of any educational enterprise should be, again with Milton, in equipping people 'to be brave men and women, worthy patriots, dear to God and famous to all ages'.

23: Too much of your educational system is driven by a warped view of status.

24: Builders and farm labourers and nurses and pay clerks are as valuable as doctors and lawyers and entrepreneurs and academics, and all of those are more valuable to your society than celebrities, be they athletes or entertainers.

25: And it should go without saying, if you thought about it, that without the farm labourers you would have no food and all else then falls.

26: The least valuable of all are layabouts; criminals and miscreants at the bottom, and the spoilt offspring of plutocrats living off wealth created by previous generations at the top.

27: One of the strangest pieces of insanity in your world is that across virtually the whole of that world, or at least, in all your settled communities, agricultural or industrial, everywhere in fact except amongst your nomadic groups, you all used to have an underclass of slaves or serfs or women, or some combination of them, forced there and held there by your cultural beliefs and theological beliefs; condemned to a miserable existence by their fellow humans.

28: And those under-classes still exist; the particular forms might have changed, but the essential oppression has not.

29: You could with your present wealth have raised them up with your vaunted education, but you have allowed your obsession with the nonsense that all people are the same to reduce and degenerate your education systems into a one size fits all system that ends up suiting nobody.

30: People are individuals, with different and varying talents, and those talents should on the one hand be identified, nurtured, and encouraged; but, on the other hand, people who hold delusional dreams that they have talents they clearly do not should be gently redirected aright.

31: Education, and spectacularly stupid theories in particular, especially in your rich west, have been largely responsible for the continuation of your unemployable underclass who do nothing but lay about drinking, smoking, watching mind-numbing television programmes that masquerade as entertainment, procreating, and thinking the world owes them a living, and they have rights and deserve Respect.

32: They do not! Respect has to be earned and rights come with concomitant responsibilities.

33: Knowledge, what you are supposed to acquire from education and study, through the use of reason and intuition, is about discovering virtue, and finding your true self.

34: Find that true self and you will then respect yourself and have the respect of others.

35: And your knowledge will then start to become wisdom.

Chapter Thirteen

1: And the people said to the Spirit; speak to us of the prophets. They seem to say different things. Did they speak truth or were they mistaken?

2: And the Spirit replied: many of the people you call prophets spoke the truth as they saw it.

3: There is not one absolute Truth in the sense that too many of you are looking for; there can be different truths for different people, and there are different truths for different times.

4: There are also different ways of interpreting the Truth, and if that sounds contradictory, it is because there can be absolutes in the spiritual realm which are not so in the material world, and apparent certainties in the material world which are not so in reality.

5: The great prophets all had glimpses of the Truth, and pronounced truths that were right for the people they spoke to, in the place and time that they lived.

6: The people have to be ready for the message that is brought to them: even if the prophet has to die for the message to begin to sink in, the people had to have been at a certain stage of development, of understanding, for the new vision to have had a chance of moving the people to the next level. The seed needs to land on fertile ground.

7: Slavery could never be, or have been, anything other than an abomination, but the early prophets said little if anything about the institution itself, only about the treatment of slaves and how the slaves themselves should behave. Were they wrong in not condemning the institution?

8: I think not: they came with a message for the times, truths that were still truths even though they were limited: the world was not ready for calls to abolish an institution that formed the bedrock of the economy.

9: The prophets were leading demands for spiritual renewal; if they had been calling for political revolution as well, their primary message, the message the world was ready to receive, would have been lost in the confusion.

10: The world had to await latter-day prophets to see the abolition of slavery.

11: The idea of the scapegoat; that the people have individually or collectively offended God, or the gods; have sinned; but that they can redress the matter by somehow transferring the sins to a goat and ceremonially driving the creature from the camp, and thereby propitiate God is, from the distance of time that you are looking at it, clearly not so much stupid as silly.

12: That concept was transferred by the early Christians to the person of Jesus; which, in thinking one man could take the due punishment for sins committed by his fellows, is not as daft as thinking a goat could, but is some ways much more offensive: a god that accepted a goat as payment is a silly god, a god that can be conned by mere mortals; but that god has then been exchanged for a god that is not only illogical and stupid but malevolent as well: what sort of god accepts punishment of the innocent in place of the guilty?

13: Nevertheless, the invention did serve a purpose.

14: The moral renewal that Jesus had called for was served far more effectively by his status as the latest incarnation of the old dying and rising god than it ever would have been if he had been seen as just another itinerant moral reformer: the devotion and sacrifice of the adherents to his supposed cause would not have been anywhere near as committed, influential and successful as they actually turned out to be.

15: The message was right for its time; but that does not make it true in perpetuity, or for any given place.

16: Truth changes with increased knowledge and advances in understanding.

17: To return to the prophets, who do you think were prophets, and what do you mean when you say someone is or was a prophet? How do you decide that one person is a major prophet or a minor prophet, or even a false prophet?

18: To take just the Christian tradition, you have your major prophets: Isaiah, Jeremiah, Ezekiel, and co. finishing with John the Baptist maybe? But before them you had Abraham and his successors through to Moses and co. and you call them Patriarchs. And between the patriarchs and the prophets you have the judges. And after your prophets you have Jesus, your messiah. And after the messiah come the disciples and the saints and apostles, then the early fathers, and then the theologians and reformers. But all these are just names you have given people.

19: Islam is no different; it just classes Jesus as a prophet and Mohammed as the last prophet.

20: And all the other religious systems have their own versions.

21: So how do you decide whether somebody is a prophet; whether what they are saying is true? Can they be right about most things, but occasionally err, or do they have to be right about everything?

22: If what they say concurs with your reason, the facility that makes you rational beings, then they can be listened to; but if their statements defy that reason, then they are wrong, and cannot be considered as prophets, no matter what they claim.

23: If someone says they have been told by God, received a message from on high; to the effect that the earth is flat; the moon is made of green cheese; a human being, any human being, is infallible; all leaders must be male, because God is male, and therefore women should be subservient to men; etcetera; then they are clearly spouting rubbish and should be treated with the contempt they deserve: they are either lunatics or charlatans, not prophets, and most certainly they have not been talking to God.

24: If someone claims to have received a revelation, revealed knowledge, from God, then it must, at the very minimum, be rational. If it is not rational then it is not of God.

25: And if it requires the consequences of the vision to be imposed on others, by force if necessary, it is definitely not of God.

26: One thing prophecy is not about is predicting the future: the future is not set and therefore cannot be foretold: those who claim to know what will occur have probably been imbibing, deliberately or otherwise, ergot ridden rye bread or magic mushrooms.

27: The great prophets, your bodhisattvas and messiahs, as you would have them; whose followers took their teachings, and used them to found new religions: Zoroaster, Miriam and Moses, Gautama, Lao-Tse, Jesus ben Joseph, Mohammed, Nanak, Baha'U'llah; are they any different from the lesser prophets, the religious reformers: Isaiah, Ezekiel, Jeremiah, Nagarjuna, and many more; or the later reformers: Maimonides, Luther, Fox, Wesley, T'ai Hsu, Gandhi, Sri Aurobindo, King, Krishnamurti, in anything other than degree?

28: They may be more important, but it is a matter of degree rather than principle.

29: But are they any different from philosophers and poets and essayists, scientists and even economists: Confucius, Aristotle, Zeno, Aurelius, Locke, Voltaire, Paine and Godwin; Ovid, Rumi, Shakespeare, Milton, Blake, Gibran and Eliot; Erasmus, Montaigne, Swift and Dostoevsky; Newton, Darwin, Einstein, Bohr and Lovelock; Smith, Hayek, Kohr and Schumacher?

30: Cannot these be considered, in their own way, even if they would themselves have rejected the term, to have been prophets?

31: They have all been messengers of God; some have had the inspired visions; been given a glimpse of Eternity; some have dreamed of a better world, and some have argued and fought for that world.

32: But could we not say the same of the great artists and musicians: Leonardo Da Vinci and Michelangelo, Mozart and Beethoven: even the odd politician might qualify: Cromwell, Wilberforce, Abraham Lincoln, Ataturk, Nehru and Nelson Mandela?

33: The list is vast, and it is a nonsense to think that visionaries stopped appearing a millennia and more ago.

34: We are then just left with the false prophets: not just the obvious crackpot sectarians, cultists and conspiracy theorists who think the world is run by aliens, or it can be saved by bouncing up and down, that medicine can be replaced by prayer, or that the world is so terrible that they must commit mass suicide: Ranters, and their modern-day successors;

35: But even more-so the megalomaniacs whose crazed theories involve saving humanity by slaughtering large numbers of their fellows: Lenin and Stalin, Hitler and Mao; the perpetrators of fraudulent pseudo-scientific theories: Marx and Freud; and last but very far from least the reactionaries who oppose progress and genuine scientific advance: the popes and ayatollahs.

36: These head-bangers are human equivalents of the sea squirt: they had a brain when they were young, but when they became old they decided they no longer needed one so they ate it.

37: It is also a nonsense, of course, to think that false prophets are only a latter day phenomena.

38: Some religious reformers may have held the beliefs they did, and acted accordingly, through the best of motives, but they may, of course, have been mistaken. They may also have been disingenuous and even nefarious.

39: The teachings of Jesus began to be modified by St Paul and the early fathers; and the process continued until they have now become corrupted to such an extent that they would be unrecognisable to the man himself if he were able to return.

40: Jesus, if he were alive today, would almost certainly not be a Christian in terms of belonging to a particular denomination;

41: In the words of Lewis Mumford; 'little men, who guarded Jesus' memory, took him, drained off the precious life blood of his spirit, mummified his body, and chained what was left in many foreign wrappings; and over these remains they proceeded to erect a gigantic tomb. That tomb is the Christian Church.'

42: The same has happened to the visions of all the bodhisattvas and prophets of all your religious systems.

43: The problem is, as usual, defined by the complications of human language: your religious institutions have used a variety of terms to describe people when it would have made more sense to use one: most of the individuals that we have been considering were, for good or ill, religious reformers.

44: Calling them prophets or apostles or theologians or philosophers or saints or poets, or even bodhisattvas and messiahs, changes nothing, and only causes confusion.

45: The same systems made things even more confusing by including on their lists of reformers people who would have been better described as politicians: reformers tend to hold to their beliefs and principles come hell or high water; politicians are restricted by what is possible, what they can sell to their constituencies, so they tend to fudge and dodge and weave at best; they need to compromise to satisfy the conflicting demands of different interests; and at their worst they are corrupt.

46: The one you call St. Paul, or the one who concocted the sayings attributed to him, and most of the early fathers in Christianity were as much politicians as they were saints and prophets and reformers.

47: The popes and ayatollahs have been, with only a few honourable exceptions, pure politicians, and corrupt ones at that; and they are joined therein by Constantine, who completed the ultimate corruption of Christianity.

48: The outstanding example of this mislabelling is, of course, Mohammed, the founder of Islam: prophets and reformers do not impose their views on others by the sword: those are the actions of a politician, and a not particularly pleasant one at that.

49: But then Islam was always as much a political system as a religious one so we should not really ever have expected anything else.

50: So how do you clear out the dross and get back to the core elements that said all that needed to be said: the different takes on the Truth, that, although expressed using slightly different terminology, are essentially always the same?

51: We are back to the constant response: you are as humans equipped with the facility of rational thought: so use it!

Chapter Fourteen

1: And the people said to the Spirit; speak to us of leadership and our political systems. Are our priests and princes and politicians all wrong? Are they all leading us astray?

2: And the Spirit replied: that is indeed far from the truth.

3: Most of your leaders are good.

4: They may be misguided, but their hearts are usually in the right place, for they usually set out with the best of motives; their desire is to improve the lot of the people they represent.

5: A very few may be corrupt from the beginning; they only purport to represent the people; their main interest being their own benefit, and yet more may find themselves corrupted by the system, subverted by their own interest or their sense of self-importance.

6: Government is by definition a necessary evil, but without it anarchy rules. It would be best if you could live in peace with each other and work together for your common benefit, but unfortunately you need some government to control your antisocial tendencies.

7: Government also implies giving up an element of personal freedom for the common good; accepting taxation to facilitate those public goods, most notably defence of the realm and the maintenance of law and order.

8: Government, above and beyond that, is even more about ensuring that the people have the capability and means to acquire sufficient food and drink to keep body and soul together.

9: Without those, government is worse than useless; nothing but an imposition.

10: It is best though if government is administered with as light a touch as is possible, and that states, national or otherwise, are on a small scale.

11: If they are so then responsibility remains, as it should, with the individual.

12: If, alternatively, they administer with a heavy hand, and are conducted on a grand scale, the individual is rendered powerless, and has more excuse for denying responsibility.

13: Larger states have a natural tendency to accrue to themselves more powers than their smaller brethren, and they also tend to be a greater threat to their neighbours: empires most often need to expand to thrive, and they can only do so by actively pursuing warfare against those neighbours.

14: Small states are most often, by dint of their size alone, unable to threaten, never mind assault, their boundary kin, and are thereby naturally inclined to be pacific.

15: Somebody said that politics is the art of the possible, and that, regrettably, is too true: politicians are inevitably beholden to their constituencies, and they are thereby often decidedly limited in their abilities to change things; their public do not like perceived cuts in services or rises in taxation, so the politicians find themselves between the proverbial rock and the hard place, trying to balance impossible demands, and with little help from the bureaucrats who stand to lose from change.

16: In addition politicians also spend so much time fighting their way to the top of the pile, and avoiding the knife in the back at the same time, that, by the time they have climbed the mountain they have often lost sight of the noble objectives they set out with.

17: To put it more colourfully, and to give a fairer assessment of their predicament, it is very difficult for someone to remember that their initial intention was to clear the swamp when they are up to their arse in alligators.

18: Your modern governments have turned into vast bureaucratic machines that have acquired a life of their own; they have become the mythical juggernaut made real; monsters that mow down anything that gets in their way.

19: In the dualism that permeates all existence they have both huge inertia, resistance to change, and unstoppable momentum; modifying your governments or their policies is like trying to halt or change the direction of a super-tanker in a moment.

20: Civil servants may try to govern in the best traditions of the service, and with the best of motives, in principle, but they have a natural interest in enhancing the power and status of their own departments, and their own salaries and pensions in the process, and a further tendency to resort to tried and tested methods, and the concomitant aversion to change, be that radical or minor.

21: You, and this you includes politicians, civil servants, and constituents, need to remove the mote from your eyes and see what you have turned yourselves into: you have made a prison for yourselves.

22: You may have allowed it to happen, and both unintentionally and with the best of intentions, but you are in chains and nobody put them on you but yourselves.

23: You have the keys though, so unlock them.

24: Freedom rules, or at least it will if you want it to!

25: Take not orders, unless you agree with them, from popes and prelates, powers and principalities, kings and queens, emperors and maharajahs, sultans and sheiks, autarchs and archimandrites, aristocrats, autocrats, plutocrats, bureaucrats, or any other sort of crat: only take orders from yourself.

26: You are sentient beings, autonomous, and answerable only to God, whatever, wherever, and however, she, he, it or they may be.

27: The only political systems that are compatible with a belief in Divinity are those based on the informed consent of the people involved. Being held responsible for one's actions necessarily requires informed consent.

28: That does not imply some sort of divine seal of approval for democracy per se, be it representative or absolute; for democracy can itself become a tyranny, unless it accepts that it is limited by the moral law as well as the laws of physics: the will of the majority is important but it cannot be regarded as an absolute determinant of what should be.

29: The transitory tastes, or judgements, or more likely misjudgements, of the general populace should not be used as an excuse to oppress harmless minorities: they are entitled under the moral law to have the freedom to determine their own futures.

30: To defer to the Americans; the authority of the people must be restrained by constitutional checks and balances to safeguard freedom and the protection of minorities.

31: As one of your greatest visionary poets, Milton, put it: 'Is it just or reasonable, that the most voices against the main end of government should enslave the less number that would be free?

32: More just it is, doubtless, if it comes to force, that a less number compel a greater to retain, which can be no wrong to them, their liberty, than that a greater number, for the pleasure of their baseness, compel a less most injuriously to be their fellow slaves.

33: Those who seek nothing but their own just liberty, have always the right to win it, whenever they have the power, be the voices never so numerous that oppose it.'

34: Others also have had wise thoughts on such matters:

35: Acton was right in saying 'Popular power may be tainted with the same poison as personal power. The will of the people cannot make just that which is unjust. All power corrupts and absolute power corrupts absolutely.'

36: And as Adam Smith almost had it: 'The statesman who should attempt to tell private individuals how to dispose of their capitals, would not only load himself with a most unnecessary burden, but assume an authority which could safely be trusted to no council or senate whatever, and which would be nowhere be so dangerous as in the hands of a man who had folly and presumption enough to fancy himself fit to exercise it.'

37: Solon had the best answer of all to the question as to which is the most perfect popular government, in terms of one built around a maxim of political morality: 'One where the least injury done to the meanest individual is considered as an insult on the whole constitution.'

Chapter Fifteen

1: And the people said to the Spirit; speak to us of war. Is it always wrong? And what about justice, and revenge, and retribution? Is capital punishment ever acceptable?

2: And the Spirit replied: all of this is politics; and just as you are hard-wired for religion, you are so too for politics: politics is a necessary evil: it is part of the human condition.

3: Politics is the only mechanism you have for resolving the practical problems you face in your day to day existence in the physical world: religion and philosophy may provide you with the underlying principles; the basic guidelines, but it is politics that mitigates the compromises you sometimes must make.

4: To paraphrase what Cromwell said to Milton: it is easy for the philosophers and poets to state what should be done, but it is the politician who has to sign the actual death warrant.

5: This is the one area where the ideas of Mohammed win over those of Gautama and Jesus; Mohammed understood that religious principles need to operate within the practical limitations imposed by the political circumstances of the material world; Gautama and Jesus would have been worse than useless as political leaders.

6: Gautama and Jesus were visionary prophets and religious reformers of the first order, whereas Mohammed was a politician with a burning desire to reform moral behaviour.

7: Unfortunately, whatever good religious ideas Mohammed had were ruined because he presumed it was necessary to impose them on others by force.

8: As to practical decisions, war is almost always disastrous, and something to be avoided if at all possible, but sometimes it may be the lesser of two evils.

9: As Wellington said; 'next to a battle lost, the greatest misery is a battle gained'.

10: On occasion, however, the actions of tyrants may be so unconscionable, so appalling, that they needs must be opposed by force of arms: the Alexanders and Caesars and Napoleons of this world will not be dissuaded from the courses they are set upon by diplomacy or argument or words of any kind.

11: However, if you have exhausted all other avenues, and are forced to resort to arms; then the fundamental moral laws place limitations on your conduct.

12: Fight, if you have to, with resolution and fortitude, as Krishna showed Arjuna, but follow the guidelines spelt out by Aquinas for a just war, but with one cavil:

13: Aquinas said that war can only be waged by a properly constituted authority, and that is correct in most circumstances; private assaults by individuals are not war, but revenge and banditry and murder.

14: It is not usually the business of a private individual to summon together the people, which has to be done in wartime, but on occasion that may be necessary.

15: The properly constituted authority receives its authority from the people it purports to represent and govern; and thereby lies the cavil: if a government abrogates the moral laws, the laws of God, and oppresses its own people, then the people have always the right to overthrow that government and replace it with a better.

16: It is, of course, best if that can be achieved by non-violent protest, but if force is the only means to rid a country of a Hitler or a Stalin, then persons who are nominally citizens of a land ruled by such, and who take up arms against their government are then participating in what must be called a legitimate war.

17: A war that is waged, be it conventional or one of popular revolt, must be a response to some grievance that needs to be rectified; some serious offence must have been given; and the response must be proportionate to the offence: if a rival group seizes the headwaters for your water supply, you may wage war to regain it; you may not seek to exterminate or enslave your enemy.

18: A just cause is required, namely that those who are attacked, should be attacked because they deserve it on account of some fault.

19: As Augustine said 'A just war is wont to be described as one that avenges wrongs, when a nation or state has to be punished, for refusing to make amends for the wrongs inflicted by its subjects, or to restore what it has seized unjustly.'

20: Then it is necessary that the belligerents should have a rightful intention, so that they intend the advancement of good, or the avoidance of evil.

21: True religion looks upon as peaceful those wars that are waged not for motives of aggrandizement, or cruelty, but with the object of securing peace, of punishing evil-doers, and of uplifting the good.

22: For it may happen that the war is declared by the legitimate authority, and for a just cause, and yet be rendered unlawful through a wicked intention.

23: To quote Augustine again: 'The passion for inflicting harm, the cruel thirst for vengeance, an unpacific and relentless spirit, the fever of revolt, the lust of power, and such like things, all these are rightly condemned in war.'

24: As for justice and retribution, you cede the control and administration of such matters to the authority of the people as a whole, subject only to the moral laws, and thereby obviate revenge and banditry, which are one and the same.

25: The essential principles behind any system of justice were laid out by Miriam and Moses centuries ago; and they have not changed: let the punishment fit the crime; and let the punishment be determined through due legal process by properly constituted authority.

26: Crimes against property merit restitution or compensation, and fines for causing nuisance.

27: Crimes against persons depend on the severity of the damage caused, and thereby varyingly merit fines, incarceration in gaol, or, in extremis, death.

28: Cruel and unusual punishments are out of order because they do not fit the crime.

29: Incarceration in perpetuity without hope of release is such a cruel punishment.

30: Tortures inflicted on miscreants are equally unacceptable because they not only degrade whatever humanity remains in the condemned, but because they also dehumanise and brutalise the inflictors of the punishment.

31: Capital punishment is something that should be determined only after considerable thought, and as a last resort, but:

32: If an individual's offence is so heinous: mass murder, serial murder or rape, and similar; and the individual concerned is judged to be likely to reoffend and is thereby a permanent danger to the public; and would thereby have to be locked up without prospect of release, then that individual is of no use, either to himself or herself, or to society or God; and the most appropriate and kindest sentence is a quick and clean death.

33: Or, to put it another way, you are just defining a product as defective, not fit for purpose, and returning it to its manufacturer.

Chapter Sixteen

1: And the people said to the Spirit; speak to us of our traditions and customs. You say they are nothing to God: are they then meaningless and valueless? Are singing and dancing and athletics pleasing to God? Are there things that displease God?

2: And the Spirit replied: they are very far from meaningless or valueless for they have meaning and value for you, and you are in a sense, as I have said, yourselves God.

3: They are only meaningless to God as All that is; and in the grand scheme of things.

4: You need holidays; a chance to rest and recuperate; and defining them from their origin as holy days, divinely ordained or not, is a good way of thinking of them.

5: You have your rites of passage; your weddings and funerals and bar-mitzvahs: these are valuable because they help you sustain a sense of community, and they allow individuals who may not be seen as particularly important by your social structures to have their day in the sun; when the social world, if only for a moment, revolves around them.

6: At a wedding the bride may be the centre of attention, the mother of the bride may be the second most important person in the room, and the groom a distant third, but the celebration is not only that; it is an opportunity for the wider community to show their support and an opportunity for wide-spread families to renew old acquaintance.

7: Funeral services provide an occasion to bid due and proper farewell to a loved one, and to recall a life; hopefully well-lived but in any event lived; and they provide solace for the relatives and friends.

8: Then you have your Christmases, Hanukah, Thanksgiving, Passover, Harvest, Solstices, Easter/Eostre, Diwali, Halloween; your religious celebrations; and these too can be good.

9: These are at their best when they act to remind you that there is an element of the divine in your community as well as in yourselves, and you only need to watch that they are not too overtaken with superstition, celebrated to excess, or used as an excuse for ostentatious display.

10: And then you have your New Year shindigs, bonfires, birthday parties, balls, barbecues and dinners.

11: There is nothing wrong with any of these, provided only that you would be advised to follow the golden rule and avoid excess; and if you slip from this then do not complain at the following day's indigestion or hangover.

12: Fasts are, on the other hand, of questionable value, unless they are of the simple form used to give the body a chance to recuperate from some sort of excess; an extension of sleep and break-fast.

13: Long term fasts undertaken as some form of perceived penance are valueless; being driven by a complete misapprehension of the nature of existence and God: if you feel you need to give up doing something, then do not give it up for Lent, just give it up altogether!

14: And please do not give up doing something you enjoy, something that gives you pleasure, because you think it will please God, or because you think there is something wrong with pleasure: that, to use a delightful piece of vernacular, is plain dumb schmuck.

15: Singing, dancing, athletics, poetry readings and thespian displays, communal or individual, all refresh the soul. Get on with them and enjoy yourselves. Even karaoke is alright: bad singing will not have you barred from paradise. And neither will bagpipes and kilts!

16: And there is nothing wrong either with a couple of glasses of fine wine to accompany a good dinner, or the port or malt whisky and cigar to wash down the coffee at the end of the meal. And the same goes for the ales consumed at the barbecue, and the pipe of tobacco or joint of marijuana on the veranda in the evening. There is the usual rider about excess of course though I am beginning to irritate myself with that constant repetition.

17: As for the roast dinner itself, or the steaks for that matter, just remember to give thanks to the essence that was the beast that gave up its life that you might feast; do not thank God unless you are thinking of Her as the beast: in Her form as the All, She neither needs nor wants your thanks.

18: This can also be seen in the visions that are best called the theology of joy and the theology of beauty.

19: God in any and all of her or his or its or their forms loves joy and beauty; for joy and beauty are love.

Chapter Seventeen

1: And the people said to the Spirit; speak to us of our relationships. What about partners, marriage, and sexual intercourse? What about friends?

2: And the Spirit replied: you are social animals; you evolved in small groups with other humans as companions and friends, and sometimes competitors and enemies.

3: You also evolved as two genders and that is the natural order of things; and the two genders are symbiotes and have need of each other.

4: Your children are divided equally in numbers of females and males, so, given the length of your lives, and the length of time that your young are vulnerable and need care, the natural order necessarily implies that you cohabit as pairs in stable relationships.

5: This is, of course, modified in two ways: since sexual intercourse is generally enjoyed by most normal humans, stronger and more powerful men have often sought and gained polygamous harems of willing or unwilling women to produce more children; and women have often sought promiscuous relationships with several alpha males in order to receive the best seed, and the consequent strong offspring.

6: Your established religions and cultural constructs have, however, always attempted to control such matters, usually to the detriment of the females, for their own nefarious purposes.

7: It was not always so, through the long period of prehistory when you were hunter gatherers, and probably only began to take place with your domestication of animals and acquisition of more property than you could carry on your backs.

8: It was only then that your males made the connection between sexual intercourse and procreation, and began to want to ensure that any property they had acquired would be passed on to their offspring and not to the offspring of another.

9: They therefore needed to ensure that their female partner had sexual intercourse with them and only them.

10: Hence began the control of women by men: sanctified, of course, by religion.

11: Here, however, nature has no opinion: he, she or it only tends to indicate a distaste for excessive promiscuity by rewarding it with sexually transmitted diseases.

12: In so far as the Universal Consciousness is concerned it is the usual response of do unto others as you would be done unto.

13: It is not just the physical consequences you need to consider though: sexual activity with others engenders strong attachments and releases powerful emotions

14: You are sexual beings and you can have a great deal of pleasure from sexual activities undertaken with no intent other than that very pleasure.

15: If sexual activities are undertaken with informed consent by whatever parties, and there are no repercussions, moral, emotional, or physical, for the participants or any other interested parties, then it can be taken that the activities have the blessing of God.

16: You only have to look at the glorious displays of the natural world for confirmation of this: the stunning variety of sexual behaviours; long term monogamies, serial monogamies, polygamies, polyandries, promiscuities and homosexual liaisons.

17: So, the only message from nature is enjoy yourselves.

18: Your religious systems may be infested with archaic prohibitions, but these are nothing but cultural hang-ups and nothing to do with God.

19: What can your reactionary old priests say to hermaphroditic sea hares that mate as both male and female simultaneously and in a tiered orgy? Or cuckoo wrasse that are all born female but change to male when achieving dominance?

20: Obsessions with prudery and prurience are signs of an inferior intellect.

21: There are no proscriptions, only the physical and emotional consequences of your choices, so do as you will.

22: And God did not say go forth and multiply and over-run the earth as a parasitic pestilence; you did! So you could breed more warriors to assault religious systems other than your own!

23: Contraception is an excellent example of your inventive talent. It enables you to choose when to have children, how many to have, and to genuinely want the ones you do have.

24: And if your population is kept at a level which the earth can sustain, then humanity has the opportunity to become, what it always should have been, a blessing to Creation rather than a curse.

25: The concept of soul-mates can also be extended, and help to explain further:

26: Aristophanes' story may have been colourful and, even allowing for poetic licence, more than a trifle eccentric, but he did have a point when he effectively suggested that soul-mates can even perform a particular symbiosis; it is not just two souls joining together to meld as one but two separated halves of one soul reuniting as one.

27: And your quest to achieve wholeness can well be expedited by that re-unification.

28: And it almost goes without saying that such partnerships can be homosexual as well as heterosexual.

29: But it goes further than that too: the relationships between soul-mates are not solely defined as sexual ones: friends, familial or otherwise, can also be soul-mates.

30: And yet further, the connection can cross species: the old adage of man's best friend being his canine companion comes to mind. Mind you, female humans cannot have diamonds as soul-mates; there are limits to the doctrine of universal consciousness!

31: Away with distractive meanderings! Souls can be brought together to work on a project, for just a short interval, or a lifetime's span, and those souls complement each other; each and every one contributing unique skills, providing inspiration, and forming a creative and supportive environment.

32: In effect you have soul groups; friends and families.

Chapter Eighteen

1: And the people said to the Spirit; you speak of the beauty of holiness. Explain to us what that means.

2: And the Spirit replied: holiness is beautiful in the sight of God, and that is necessarily so, for it is a reflection of the nature of God.

3: For God as existence is holy and beautiful, and you are the same.

4: But there is external beauty and the beauty of the light that dwells within.

5: There is beauty in form, both artificial and natural.

6: But the beauty of holiness is greater than the beauties of time and sense and it differs so much from the beauties of mere nature: in actuality, Holiness is the ultimate form of beauty.

7: The universe has beauty on the grand scale: stars and galaxies and nebulae.

8: It has beauty on the microscopic scale: snowflakes and plankton and atoms.

9: Your world has beauty in the vistas of nature: its oceans and deserts, its mountains and forests, its clouds and sunsets, its tempests and volcanoes.

10: You wonder at its mammals and birds, fish and cetaceans, reptiles and insects, find yourselves rapt before the vistas of its lovely glens and peaks, and lose yourselves in the sounds of the softly babbling brook and the breeze rustling the trees, and the scent of the flowers.

11: It has beauty in your artifices: your cottages and farms, your cathedrals and temples, your bridges and trains.

12: You have beauty in your art and music and literature, your sculptures and paintings, your sonatas and choirs of angels.

13: You have beauty in your ideas and science.

14: But all of these are as nothing compared to the beauty of God, and that is the beauty of holiness.

15: They are as nothing before the love that is within you; the beauty of the spiritual graces.

16: And you fail to discern that which is of the highest value to God.

17: You, and the God that is within you, must remove the scales from your eyes and ears, and then you will perceive that holiness is the true form of beauty.

18: The beauty of holiness is rooted in your inner being; it is the light within you.

19: The beauties of the world are but vanities, but the beauty of holiness is spiritual and Divine.

20: The beauty of holiness abides forever, and again therefore differs radically from all the beauties of the earth.

21: They are transient and ephemeral, as is all physical existence.

22: Your cathedrals, temples and palaces erode away to nothing; your paintings and tapestries are eaten up by decay.

23: The beauties of the autumnal shades are blown from the woods with the winds of winter.

24: The peerless sunsets, and lovely moonlit nights, which far excel all human works, vanish from sight before your eyes.

25: The fairest human countenance withers all too quickly with the passage of time, and all is consumed in the grave.

26: That old hymn again, and right this time; 'change and decay in all around I see'.

27: The beauty of holiness satisfies in a way that they cannot, and hence it is fundamentally different from the external beauty of entities of time and space.

28: Eventually all such either pall for you or you realise they are not enough.

29: So as with gold and all the things of your world they lose their lure when you realise what you truly are: build not and gather not treasures on this earth; seek only the treasures that are eternal.

30: Consider the traveller who treads all the points of the compass, seeking new experiences.

31: As many as there may be, none can truly give contentment of mind and peace of heart.

32: You are so much more than just material creatures, and you well know that; your inner yearnings tell you so, and you therefore also know that you need more than just material things, even if they are beautiful, to satisfy your needs.

33: The only beauty which fades not and lasts forever is the beauty of holiness.

34: Remember the old story of the bull terrier, ugliness personified, but faithful to the end, and chosen as a companion to a man's children precisely to show them that you do not have to be beautiful to love and be loved.

35: Remember also that the origin of beauty began in the holiness of silence and to that holiness of silence all beauty shall return.

36: And thus it is that you oft find the holiness of beauty, not so much in ceasing to make noise, but in the ambient silence of the night, and the quietude of retreat.

37: The sound of silence is the starlight that formed you and to which you are destined to return;

38: Hence and therewith is also the peace that passes understanding; be still, and know God.

39: The cares and vicissitudes of your world too often blind you to the peace that lives within you, so open your heart and realise the presence of the love that is the Eternal Consciousness.

40: For the fruits of the Spirit endure forever, and the love therein shall last long after your poor world has turned to dust and is but a memory in the Eternal Consciousness.

41: And it is the things of God, your connection to the Eternal Consciousness, and the love within you, which alone afford satisfaction.

42: For God is our infinite delight. God is the source of our greatest and purest joy. God dissolves us and creates us again from within. God touches us and draws us beyond ourselves into an ecstasy of love and infinite possibility.

43: And to come to understand God as beauty requires stillness and depth. It means discovering your own mystery; learning your own depth. For only what is deep can love. Shallowness has no time for anything but itself.

44: You are too much concerned with action and purposes and ends.

45: You need to do to survive, but you need to be to live. Doing without being is only existing.

46: Being involves being able to see and realise the beauty of God and know that it is within you.

47: And you need stillness to see the beauty of God.

48: God speaks with the small still voice, and we need silence, be that meditation or prayer, and the absence of our own voice as much as external noise to be able to hear that voice.

49: And to poach from Gladstone, the 'inner citadel', which is, and ever was, the still small voice, the private conscience, remains perpetually impregnable, because it is 'the vice-regent of God on earth'.

Chapter Nineteen

1: And the people said to the Spirit; should we always proclaim what we believe to be the truth? Is it ever right to tell lies?

2: And the Spirit replied: As Pilate said; 'What is truth?' There is the Eternal Truth and there is the truth that is yours and yours alone, and the truths that are probabilities.

3: Much of your time and invention is spent denying the latter because you do not understand the first two.

4: As bankers and entrepreneurs and traders and salesmen you bend the truth to keep your enterprises 'competitive'; as politicians you deny the truth if you cannot 'sell it' to your constituency: Churchill's 'terminological inexactitudes'.

5: You may know in your heart of hearts what you need to do, how to deal with the pain and suffering you inflict on each other, and on yourselves: your prophets and gurus and philosophers have told you how to solve the problems, but your refusal to contemplate short term inconvenience always holds sway, from generation to generation, seemingly without end: you are, in truth, lying to yourselves.

6: You dislike uncertainty, yet uncertainty is the core of existence; it is uncertainty that is the Truth; and the certainties you seek are naught but fantasies and chimeras.

7: And because things are never certain, you are required to hold opinions, interpret matters and make decisions, and you do not like having to do that either.

8: And your behaviour is too often determined not by what happens to you but by how you interpret the events.

9: Following some unpleasant occurrence or even disaster, some of you relapse into defeat and despair, seeing it as some form of deserved punishment, but others treat it as a challenge to be overcome.

10: Your decisions follow your interpretations.

11: Your problem is that not only do you find it difficult to accept the truth that uncertainty rules all, but you also dislike taking responsibility for yourselves.

12: You are happier when you think you can blame circumstance.

13: The uncertainty that drives existence also drives the processes by which your brain 'thinks'.

14: You think you know what is real and what is not, but in truth 'your reality' is personal to you, and unique to you; it is 'a reality' that has been constructed by the interpretations that have been created by your mind.

15: Because this 'reality' is unique to you, you are, in effect, all alone in your own little world.

16: And because happenstance can unfortunately deconstruct or invalidate your reality, that 'reality', which you have invested so much capital in, can appear threatened.

17: So you begin to lie to yourself, because you are afraid you do not have the ability to face up to what is not just a new circumstance but a new you.

18: Then you begin to lie to others; the 'white lies' that obviate the problems caused when telling people the truth might upset them, and you are happier when other people like you.

19: You do not like the feeling that your world is chaotic and disordered: you build a survival mechanism where you construct a make-believe world of control and order.

20: Then you delude yourselves over the problems facing your societies, your species as a whole, and your wider world: you hope that if you ignore them they will go away, but they will not of course.

21: Truth, in contrast, is normally founded on evidence.

22: The real core of your problem is that, despite your distaste for it, the truths of your physical existence, as with all else, are always approximations.

23: Existence itself is probabilistic; the absolute certainty you crave is a fantasy.

24: Telling lies to yourselves allows you to indulge in the illusion that your personal worlds are safe and complete, and that you are not going to be overwhelmed by the fear attached to living in a reality that is ultimately incomprehensible.

25: You cannot escape uncertainty, and if you wish to achieve enlightenment, you need to meet it face to face, and accept existence for what it is.

Chapter Twenty

1: And the people said to the Spirit; speak to us of justice and mercy. It is said that God is both just and merciful, but surely justice and mercy are incompatible? You can surely only be just or merciful, not both?

2: And the Spirit replied; justice and mercy in the sense that your language treats them as incompatible are human concepts, and nothing to do with God as the Universal Consciousness.

3: You are once again under a misapprehension.

4: Justice is a legal concept, and implies consequential punishment.

5: Mercy is a moral response relating to the ability to forgive.

6: It therefore does indeed seem, on the face of it, that you cannot have both at the same time.

7: My answer, as usual, relates to the duality at the core of existence.

8: If I use the physical world as an analogy, the cause and effect mechanism at the heart of the physical laws are the equivalent of the justice part of the moral laws.

9: The susceptibility to pneumonia that you acquire in old age is an effect with a cause, and is therefore just, but it used to be known, and with good reason, as the old person's friend, and is the tempering of justice with mercy.

10: Your human societies need laws to deal with disputes between individuals, and that is a necessary consequence of your nature: most of you behave most of the time, some of you behave some of the time, and a few behave all the time; but until you all fit the last category, then you need law.

11: You then deal with miscreants, and justice is when the punishment fits the crime.

12: Justice can be tempered with mercy, and that, in moral terms, is forgiveness.

13: Can you forgive others, can you ask for forgiveness from others, and can you, when you need to, forgive yourself?

14: And God as the Universal Consciousness, and of which you are both part and whole, is party to both cause and effect and justice, and forgiveness and mercy.

Chapter Twenty One

1: And the people said to the Spirit; speak to us of dying. What of suicide and euthanasia and abortion?

2: And the Spirit replied: Death seems to deny the future, and to deny life, and human beings have coped with this in various ways.

3: In the early stages of humanity's cultural and intellectual evolution, almost a pre-personal stage, the problem you have with death did not exist since archaic man was not aware of the passage of time in the way that you are.

4: As humans started to become self-conscious, to acquire egos, it was only then that the temporal sense came into being.

5: During the Dreaming ages though, deep into historical time, and still yet through to the present for many; your resonance with and connection to the natural cycles of existence, together with your hopes for resurrection or reincarnation, the continuation of your personal existence after death, have tranquilised, if not completely banished, your fear of death.

6: Now, though, when you are now properly aware of your true mortality, and the mortality of the very cosmos itself, the eventual demise of existence and the end of time, you are afraid.

7: But fear not, for Death too has purpose; it is not a meaningless end to a pointless existence; it simply sees you merging with Donne's dazzling darkness and noisome silence.

8: Dying is only the process through which you reach the gate of death.

9: The physical body changes constantly throughout its existence: some parts grow and continue to grow; some parts wear out and fall off and are replaced; some parts die and are not replaced.

10: What is certain is that the body ages and eventually dies.

11: It may die suddenly due to the catastrophic failure of a vital organ, a heart attack or a stroke; it may die slowly through disease, a cancer; or quickly through the same, ebola or the plague; or it may die very slowly, fade away as it were, through the slow failure of its parts.

12: It may die peacefully or it may die in great pain. It will die though.

13: The physical body however is not all there is; there is the essence, the spark of the divine spirit, the individual consciousness, the soul if you will, and the fusion of the two make up the whole which is you.

14: When the physical body dies, the divine spark departs and returns to the Universal Consciousness, and leaves behind a mere cadaver that is destined to decay and be recycled to its mother, the earth.

15: However, just as the cadaver is of no use to the departed soul, or for that matter, to the surviving relatives, there are also points and circumstances in life where the spark, the spirit, whatever you choose to call it, has clearly departed the corporeal body, but the body still continues to exist, nothing but a shell; and the corollary, probably sadder still, where the soul, the spark, is still present, but the body is a crippled and blasted remnant, effectively a prison for the spirit.

16: This is a function of the circumstance where your science, your medicine, has marched ahead of your ethical understanding and your theological understanding, and this is not in the natural order of things; it is not as it should be.

17: You treat death as if it were some sort of defeat, an affront both to your obsession with existence and your technological skill; and not as it is; part and parcel with life.

18: There is nothing to be gained by obstinately clinging on to life when it is clearly time to go; let go; and if you cannot, let someone else help you on the way.

19: In principle there is nothing wrong with suicide, assisted suicide or euthanasia; everything depends on the circumstance.

20: If you have reached an advanced age, have a body with worn out parts that cannot be replaced, are in constant pain, are a burden on others, and have done everything you need to do and want to do; then settle your affairs, make your farewells, have a good last meal and a bottle of wine, then settle down, consume some narcotics and drift off listening to your favourite music.

21: You are not rushing uninvited into the presence of God; you are God and it is you who are issuing the invitation.

22: It is your choice to go, or equally not to go yet.

23: For those who are no longer capable of acting, when the spirit is there but the body is not, then others should render assistance out of compassion: you do not allow dogs to suffer needlessly, so why do you do less for your fellow humans?

24: For those who are no longer capable of making a decision, but are in the unenviable position where the body is there but the spirit has departed, then you should construct the mechanisms in your societies to take the decision on their behalf.

25: It is surely not beyond the wit of your courts and medics to ensure the necessary cavils and safeguards, and arrive at a decision that is both dispassionate and compassionate.

26: At the very least your hospitals and clinics could follow the old maxim of Arthur Clough; 'You shall not kill, but need not strive, officiously, to keep alive.'

27: Much the same principles can be applied to abortion.

28: If a woman is pregnant with a foetus that is seriously disabled or damaged, and which, if carried to term, would likely have a short, painful, and probably pointless existence, then she does no wrong by choosing to have an abortion.

29: And it is the decision of the woman; she it is who carries the burden and the pain; she might choose to consult her partner and family, but that would be entirely up to her; and it would be damned impertinent for someone not connected to her to even presume to comment, never mind condemn.

30: Idiot priests, fundamentalist maniacs, mad old bats and meddlesome lawyers should be told to shut the proverbial up!

31: Even if it is the case that the foetus is healthy; then if it is being carried by a woman who already has half a dozen children who she is struggling to feed, and the extra mouth would threaten the survival of the whole family; then too she is not to be condemned for opting for an abortion.

32: If you think that personal morality can be separated from matters that affect the biosphere of which you are part then you are seriously mistaken; you are spiritually part of the Cosmos as a whole, and that will continue with or without you, but you cannot damage the biosphere you depend on for your physical survival and still expect your physical existence to continue.

33: I repeat, as individual humans your existence may count as a blessing, but if your numbers grow too great then that blessing will become a curse, and limiting your numbers, even by abortion, suicide and euthanasia, is better than the alternative.

34: Your ancestors knew this; when someone grew too old and slow, and could no longer keep up, they knew their continued existence threatened the survival of their children and grandchildren: they left the camp and wandered off into the desert or the snow: Oates; 'I am going outside and shall be some time.'

35: And that is not counting those who lay down their lives for others: 'Greater love hath no man'.

36: And when you have gone, what have you left behind and what has gone on?

37: All that you have left behind is a corpse, a mere cadaver, for your relatives to deal with.

38: For you that survive, say goodbye to your dear departed with what ceremony you will, and then dispose of the cadaver cleanly and quickly, and without wasting valuable land on it, never mind constructing a Mausoleum in remembrance of it.

39: Such ostentation is of no use whatever to the corpse, and only helps the relatives to carry on wallowing in their grief.

40: The present and the future are for the living not for the dead.

41: There will not be a physical resurrection of the body; the very idea is a nonsense: what body are you expecting to come back to?

42: If you died at an advanced age are you hoping for your body as it was at its physical peak? And are you expecting that the mind in that body will have all your memories of all your years? But that your intellect will no longer be doddery?

43: And if you died as an infant are you hoping that you will be resurrected as the adult you were intended to become?

44: In both cases you would not be you.

45: And what is the you that is to be resurrected; you are not the same person you were five minutes ago, never mind a year ago.

46: And that ignores cluttering up an already overpopulated earth with vast numbers of immortal resurrected dead! As I said; nonsense!

47: Your essence, your spirit, returns on death to the Universal Consciousness, to God, and though still conscious of its physical existence, it is also conscious of all else.

48: Your essence and spirit may also, or may not, as the case may be, be reincarnated to another physical existence; you may decide that you need to experience more to further enhance, or even complete, your understanding;

and you equally might, or may, for they are one and the same, not reincarnate.

49: It is, as always, your choice.

50: Much of your problem with dying is connected to your desire to hang on to life to the bitter end; your genes are hot wired to seek your continued survival:

51: And if and when you are forewarned by medical prognosis of your impending demise you typically respond sequentially with denial, the diagnosis must be wrong; anger, why me, I do not deserve this; bargaining, let me live God and I promise to do something I think You want me to do; acceptance, a final and sensible acknowledgement of reality.

52: Death is just another part of the experiment you are partaking in, and just as you create your own life in conjunction with the Universal Consciousness, you also create your death.

53: It may even be that holding on till an end that appears unedifying, and even decidedly unpleasant, could serve a purpose: you may need to relinquish your apparent ability to control things, and the pride that goes with that; to allow others to minister to you.

54: And what you do is as always your choice.

Chapter Twenty Two

1: And the people said to the Spirit; speak to us of time, for we do not understand.

2: And the Spirit replied: time is of two forms; clock time and psychological time, chronos and kairos, your time and God's time.

3: Chronological time is the simple form, the measuring of the motion of the planets and all else in your physical world; your seconds and milliseconds and microseconds, your minutes and hours, your days and weeks and months and years, your centuries and millennia and aeons.

4: It is the time you use to regulate your daily lives; to determine your working week; to arrange your appointment with the dentist; and so on.

5: It constitutes your remembrance of things past, and enables you to make probabilistic predictions of the future: sunrise will be at a particular time tomorrow;

6: This time flows in only one direction; you can predict that if you throw a cricket ball at a window it will take one second to arrive and will then probably shatter the pane; you can also say that if that occurs, you cannot reverse time; reassemble the shards of glass and cause the cricket ball to retrace its path to your hand.

7: It is in this sense that you think of time as a dimension, in the same way that you think of space in terms of its having three dimensions, but all of this is, in reality, an illusion.

8: God's time, kairos, is the time between times, the point where the past and the future meet in an undefinable and eternal now.

9: This is time in its psychological sense; a function of consciousness, and a probability.

10: Matter or energy, and they, of course, are only different facets of the same thing, genuinely exist, in that they can be independently measured; where a particle is, and what it is doing, its position and momentum, however, are dependent upon each other, are inextricably linked, and cannot be measured independently or separately.

11: They are only probabilities, and as the accuracy with which you measure one improves, so the accuracy with which you can determine the other declines.

12: And momentum is determined by that ephemerality; time.

13: For some things; photons, and non ageing bacteria, the basic building blocks of the universe, time does not exist in any meaningful sense.

14: For a photon, the end of the universe has already arrived and the beginning is still here, because it is a timeless entity. It was born at the beginning of time, and exists unchanged in an ever-continuing now until the end of time. It has neither past nor future, it just is.

15: The nature of a photon does not change, though the frequency of its energy might.

16: Bacteria too are ageless in the sense that individual cells have the potential to maintain their structure indefinitely. They do not age; individual cells may be killed by toxins, heat, cold, dehydration, ultra-violet radiation, etc, but they do not grow old.

17: Such microscopic creatures reproduce by cloning, parthenogenesis; each daughter cell is a carbon copy of its parent, and the whole bacterial cell is effectively immortal.

18: As an aside, if Jesus had been born by parthenogenesis, through a virgin birth, he would have been a clone and a girl.

19: As we ascend the scale of life though, organisms increasingly abandon cloning in favour of sexual reproduction, and creatures that reproduce sexually have, for their species, set maxima for their life-spans; they have genetically determined parameters fixed by natural selection.

20: You have a world and a universe with both ageless and mortal cells, entities whose existence is determined in and by time, and entities for whom time is meaningless.

21: The difference between ageless and mortal cells is because the copying of DNA is seldom perfect: mistakes sometimes creep in, so you have an existence which is asymmetric.

22: These mistakes can be rectified by deleting the mutation, but only with significant costs to the energy budget of the cell.

23: Single celled microscopic life-forms such as bacteria, and half-life entities such as viruses can settle the bill without difficulty because they are organised, designed, constructed for optimum efficiency.

24: More complex creatures, however, are unable to settle that bill; the cost has become too high; if it was able to clear undesirable mutations out of the system, the creature would have become uncompetitive.

25: In effect, during evolution, complex life gave up immortality in exchange for cost efficiency; a novel solution to the problem of reproduction was found: a survival machine with an inbuilt self-destruct mechanism: a perishable, throwaway body with a maximum use by date.

26: This perishable body built by genes contains a perishable brain as well though, and for you this is the vehicle for your sense of self, your sense of 'I am', your ego.

27: When the ego was born, death entered consciousness.

28: If the mythical 'Fall', the entry of the serpent into Eden, means anything then this is it.

29: It is also the point at which you started to become conscious of the passage of time, mere illusion though it is.

30: For your convenience you divide time into past, present, and future, but this is entirely an artifice.

31: God, as a discrete entity, is unchanging because there is no time passage for God; past, present and future are one and the same thing; they are simultaneous not consecutive

32: God as the cosmos, on the other hand, changes and grows

33: For you, with the rest of the cosmos, the only constant is change.

34: The past has gone, the future is only a probability until it becomes present, and the present cannot be defined other than as a mathematical construct, an abstraction: it belongs with other similars, zero and infinity.

35: This present is the meeting point of the future with the past, as a tangent touches a circle, and it is no more measurable than infinity or zero

36: It is a flux in which the mind is simultaneously a memory of the immediate past and an open invitation for that which is immediately to come, a dream of time which flows both ways.

37: And in the world of fundamental particles, the 'real world', time does flow both ways, from the future to the past as from well as the past to the future:

38: But time does not really flow at all; that is just an illusion of the human mind.

39: Time does not move: the illusion that it does is replaced in reality by your individual self voyaging, by virtue of the choices you make, among the hills and dales of a future space-time that is already here.

40: In the material world again, space-time is curved, so if you were to travel in any direction for a sufficient period of clock time you would return to the point you started from; there is nothing 'outside' the universe, which is expanding into nothing.

41: As a consequence of this, you have a Universe which consists of a finite quantity of matter and energy but is set within a framework of space-time which is expanding to dissipation.

42: And bar that, in truth, there cannot be any absolute prediction of the future, for the future is not determined; it is only a probability, and there is always an element of uncertainty; there is no foreknowledge, for God or anything else.

43: Of course, the existence of God cannot be contingent upon anything.

44: But God cannot exist without a concomitant matching existence of intelligence and sentience, or, if She did, Her existence would be pointless, or at least unbelievably tedious.

45: Other beings that are sentient and intelligent must therefore exist coterminously alongside God; or, to put it another way, God has multiple personalities.

46: Either there was a time when God as a singular personality existed alone; pointless and tedious as above, or time does not exist for God.

47: Psychological time, the framework of space-time, is God's time.

48: And it is in the sense that you, the Eternal you, the real you, are God, that time does not exist for you either.

49: In the words of T. S. Eliot; 'To apprehend the point of intersection of the timeless with time, is an occupation for the saint, (or the lunatic and there is not much between them); no occupation either, but something given and taken, in a lifetime's death in love, ardour and selflessness and self-surrender'.

Chapter Twenty Three

1: And the people said to the Spirit; speak to us of this life, and whereby God is everything individually and everything together, for we would know more.

2: And the Spirit replied:

3: Microscopic organisms are 'alive', in the same way that you are; individually they take in energy, excrete it as waste, and reproduce.

4: But the mechanisms that drive these microscopic are just physics; cells and DNA move in the classical world, as defined and described by classical mechanics;

5: Their constituent parts are just protons and neutrons and electrons, or if you would break it down further, various sub-atomic particles; bosons, gluons, muons, tau, quarks, photons, and neutrinos, the motion of which is described by quantum mechanics; and that too is just physics.

6: But microscopic organisms can also operate collectively; together they can construct new forms of 'life' which have self purpose.

7: These new collective forms of life can age, have memories and desires; but they are still at their core just a collection of cells:

8: What you have is effectively a form of magic.

9: This even applies to conglomerations of atomic and sub-atomic particles, which combine to form 'dead' collectives; for example the Sun.

10: You can also have conglomerations of collective forms forming grand collectives: corals, pando aspen trees, stromatolites, and colonies of social insects, ants and bees, with their effective hive mind.

11: This 'life' is special; it has become more than the sum of its parts, be they elements, cells, or whatever.

12: And just as you, with your intellects, are special, so too are all the other forms of life.

13: You too often think, however, that you are extra-special, simply because of that intellect, but in truth other forms of life have intellect as well:

14: Consider only the anthropoid apes, cetaceans, cephalopods, pachyderms, and crows, pigs and dogs:

15: If you in your hubris destroy yourselves, and in the process do not manage to take them with you, they might well evolve to succeed you.

16: The ultimate form of this life is the universe, the grand collective of everything.

17: And the more complex the organism, the greater are its capabilities.

18: And for God, who is all of this and more, the capability is beyond comprehension.

Chapter Twenty Four

1: And the people said to the Spirit; tell us more of this existence, for it seems to be confusing and contradictory and we do not understand.

2: And the Spirit replied: the whole of existence is a Duality and a series of dualities:

3: In the physical realm you have the wave-particle dual nature of light, the equivalence between energy and matter, the existence of antimatter to counter matter, and the essential and irreducible interconnection between space and time.

4: You also have the determinism of the neurons that drive all the mechanisms within your own bodies which nevertheless culminates in the beings that you are with your free will.

5: Then you have a world where, courtesy of the understanding of Heisenberg, the accuracy with which you can determine the position of any given particle necessarily reduces the accuracy with which you can determine its momentum.

6: And yet again it would seem existence is both probabilistic and deterministic at one and the same time:

probabilistic in the microscopic realm, in the world of quantum mechanics, and in the everyday world of normal time, and deterministic in the macroscopic realm, the world of relativity, and at the beginning and the end of cosmic creation.

7: And if we move to the half world between the material and spiritual realms where esoteric mathematical notions rule, then you have the dispute between finity and infinity.

8: Shifting then on to the spiritual realm, you have the dualities of good and evil, pleasure and suffering, and matter and spirit.

9: Then you have the determinism of fate, the omniscience of God in other words, versus the freewill that is the necessary concomitance of responsibility, and the knowledge that God is both transcendent and immanent at the same time.

10: And if you want the final confusions you have God as both the whole of existence and as a discrete entity that is separate from existence; God that exists and God that does not, and a cosmos where time runs from beginning to end in an ever present now.

11: And for all of these the whole is greater than the sum of the parts.

12: This is not to say that the duality of existence is symmetrical: there is more matter than antimatter in the universe; life itself is made up of imperfections, the mutations involved during reproduction for starters; and returning to theology, the God that is all, the Universal Consciousness is more present than the God that is everything that is not.

13: Then the wave-particle duality is a probability relationship; there is no 'real' thing that both moves as a particle and propagates as a wave: the wave properties are actually only probability distributions connected to abstract, 'non-real', particles, which are only revealed in statistical distributions of concrete, 'properly real', particles.

14: And there is yet more to come: it is possible that there is no world independent of observers: you are living with Alice in her Wonderland where cats, Cheshire or otherwise, have grins but no substance, and in her Looking Glass where we stare out and see only ourselves looking back in; an existence where we are a figment of our own imagination.

15: It is also possible that there is a physical reality which is actually observer-independent; but as per usual that is not the end; there is the probabilistic problem for conventional existence: you could have an alternative universe created for all given eventualities; and this is not just a new universe when you choose between cereal and fruit or both for breakfast, but a new universe for each event at the quantum level, the multiverse, the maximum number of universes possible;

16: Or you could have a reality which is modified by the 'will' of quanta; a world where it is not the observer of an event but the observed event itself that determines the outcome; in effect an electron chooses its own state;

17: Or yet again it could be that reality is modified by consciousness;

18: In the physical world it seems that the very act of observation changes the phenomenon being observed: for us to be able to detect an electron, a photon must first interact with it, and this interaction will change the path of that electron.

19: For a more practical example; in thermodynamics, a standard thermometer must absorb some thermal energy to record a temperature, and this thereby changes the temperature of the body which it is measuring.

20: If you want the theological and or philosophical version, then you should revert to the classic options; the three alternative explanations and possible cause of existence: existence has been created by a self explanatory creator being, God, which by now you should know is you; existence is accidental and has no purpose, it just is; or existence is not real, it does not actually exist but is only a figment of something's imagination.

21: The physical realm's counterpart of the theological imaginary realm, if that is not a particularly demented oxymoron, is obvious.

22: The multiverse and a reality which is modified by events are clearly counterparts of the theological accident; if correct they would be constructing a pointless existence.

23: The multiverse and a reality which is modified by events could in theory have been formed by a self explanatory creator being, but you would then have a god who would be responsible for constructing a pointless existence, a pointless god.

24: The only sensible conclusion is that consciousness is at the core of everything: it is the observer, God, God in us, and us in God that determines the event.

25: And consciousness is not just an observer but is an active participant in the workings of the world: mind and matter, subject and object can no longer be considered separate things; sublimely and subtly, they interact.

26: It is consciousness, literally and factually, that creates reality by summoning forth material particles, definable certainties, from the elusive quantum wave.

27: The whole basis of matter dissolves into an intangibility that is wraithlike; the quantum wave is a mathematical construct, only a ripple in the realms of possibility, until someone or something looks at it: it is only when an observer intrudes that the particle becomes real.

28: And the traces of all that has ever been in the universe still exist, locked in the fabric of space-time, and in the mind of God.

29: Nature is parsimonious: She loses nothing and wastes nothing; energy and matter may be transformed but in total they are conserved.

30: Your human lives, the most spectacular example, as far as you yet know, of matter in the universe, cannot be an exception to the law of preservation of all things and events in the cosmos.

31: All the experiences, in all their breadth and depth, of someone's life do not vanish without a trace but remain encoded in the energy flows of the Cosmos, locked in the core of reality, the Mind of God; for God experiences them with you.

32: And existence encodes in its duality both order and chaos, and the movement between them.

33: If you look at it one way then the material existence has moved from order to disorder: at the beginning the Cosmos was in a highly ordered state, a unity of particulate matter and energy, but with the passage of time, in the sense that time does actually pass, it will reach a state at the end of total disorder; a position where the resulting energy has no information available to enable it to be converted in systems from one form to another.

34: Alternatively, and of equal validity, the material existence has moved from chaos to order: the construction of atoms, then simple molecules, and complex molecules, to arrays of the same in the evolution of life-forms: life defies cosmic chaos by constructing self-replicating patterns which repair and replace themselves: life both draws energy and information from its environment and returns them to it. This is the true Samsara.

35: God as everything that is; energy, matter, the cosmos, evolves and changes in the movement from one form to another, but in another sense does not change because the total amount of energy in the cosmos is a fixed quantity.

36: God as everything that is not does not change: as a discrete entity, God is space and time and space time; the framework around which the cosmos is built.

37: Time and space and space time are no more creations than God is; except in the sense that God and time and space and space time, for they are one and the same, creates Itself.

38: God as 'everything that is' is finite, God as 'everything that is not' is infinite.

39: God as 'everything that is' is rational, God as 'everything that is not' is irrational.

40: God as 'everything that is' is the alpha and the omega, God as 'everything that is not' is both infinity and zero.

41: Like Schrodinger's cat God is alive and dead at the same time; the decision of the observer, be that you or God, to open the box summons forth the real cat, dead or alive, from its ghostly quantum state of non-being.

42: To put it another way, 'Reality/Existence' is chaotic and by definition non-deterministic.

43: The God that is synonymous with that Reality/Existence; the God that exists and is real is chaotic and non-deterministic: It, She, He does not have a plan; the future is not set; you as part of that chaotic reality are free to determine your own future.

44: Non-Reality/Non/Existence is ordered and by definition deterministic.

45: The God that is not is synonymous with that Non-Reality/Non-Existence; the God that does not exist and is not real is ordered and deterministic; It, She, He does have a plan; the future is set.

46: When the Universe ends, as it will, Existence/Reality will end with it, and the God that is will die with it.

47: All that will remain is Non-existence, and the God that does not exist; that is the framework that is space time, which cannot die, because though it can only be measured and determined in the presence of Existence, it is not part of that Existence, and also not contingent on that Existence.

48: The God that is not, the God that does not exist, may then, at a time that cannot be measured or determined, because there is no existence to measure it by, create or re-create a new Existence/Reality, a new form of itself, the true Creatio ex Nihilo.

Chapter Twenty Five

1: And the people said to the Spirit; what then are you? If existence is an illusion are you something that is appearing to us as an hallucination? Tell us for we are now thoroughly confused.

2: And the Spirit replied: I am immaterial but nevertheless still real.

3: In the sense that I am without mass; am energy without mass, you could argue that I am not part of your reality.

4: But then our universe contains mass-less particles, and they are still real.

5: With you, I am part and all of the Universal Consciousness, one with the God that is all.

6: Ultimately though I am an out-flowing, an effulgence from God in the form of God as everything that is not.

Chapter Twenty Six

1: And the people said to the Spirit; tell us more of the Lord God, for we do not understand. Surely the Lord God is all-powerful, all-knowing, and all-seeing? And some claim the Earth itself is our God; is that true?

2: And the Spirit replied: the total amount of energy in the Cosmos is finite.

3: If the Universe were infinite in terms of energy as well as in the expanding fabric that is space-time, then that is the same as having an infinity of infinities; in other words all possibilities actually exist.

4: If all possibilities were to exist then everything that could occur will occur, or, in psychological time, is currently occurring.

5: If that is the case, then our actions have every possible consequence; whatever we do does not matter; there is no moral consequence.

6: If that were so there would be no point to existence.

7: If you are content to accept a pointless existence, then I am nought but a chimaera, a figment of your imagination, and a dream, and God does not exist in any form.

8: But as I said, the total amount of energy in the Cosmos is finite, and the universe is both sensible and purpose-full.

9: The amount of energy may change between forms, and between energy and what you call matter, but the total amount was created at the beginning of time and neither increases nor diminishes.

10: In the sense then that God and the Cosmos are One, God is both unchanging and constantly changing.

11: This dichotomy is built into the fabric of existence: at the microscopic level where the effects of quantum mechanics apply, existence is entirely probabilistic; and at the macroscopic level, existence is ultimately predetermined and predestined.

12: God as 'Everything that is' is part of that probability at the microscopic level and also part of that predestination on the grand scale, and not above and beyond it.

13: To talk in terms of what existed before the beginning is incoherent: time and space came into existence at the beginning as God created Herself and Himself; and the matter and energy that constitute and expanded to form the Cosmos, were created simultaneously; Existence, in all its forms, created Itself.

14: That energy and matter, however, make up the physical universe, everything that is, and therefore God as Everything that is; whereas space and time are the framework around and through which the physical universe is measured; they are not things, and are therefore God as Everything that is not.

15: You cannot have 'a before the beginning of time', apart from the conception of God as 'Everything that is not'.

16: God in that sense is, of course, necessarily unchanging.

17: God is only omnipotent, all-powerful, in terms of God as 'Everything that is not', and it is in this sense, and only in this sense, that we can consider God to be a discrete Entity, separate from Creation.

18: God as 'Everything that is', the Cosmos itself, Existence and the force that flows through it and sustains it, cannot be all-powerful because Existence has been set on a path, and the laws of physics that drive it are determined, so Existence will run its course to the end of time.

19: God as 'Everything that is' cannot change that.

20: In addition God as 'Everything that is' cannot be omniscient in the sense of all-seeing, or all-knowing, for the details of the future are not set.

21: As Existence changes, and evolves, so does God.

22: Existence as a totality of energy will continue until it dissipates as heat or collapses back in on itself.

23: It will then cease to exist, it will die, and God as 'Everything that is' will die with it.

24: It goes almost without saying that humanity as discrete physical beings, and the world they think of as theirs, will have long predeceased that event.

25: With Krishnamurti you can stare into the abyss and see yourself looking out.

26: As Shakespeare's Macbeth had it; 'To-morrow, and to-morrow, and to-morrow, creeps in this petty pace, from day to day, to the last syllable of recorded time, and all our yesterdays have lighted fools the way to dusty death. Out, out, brief candle! Life's but a walking shadow, a poor player that struts and frets his hour upon the stage, and then is heard no more: it is a tale told by an idiot, full of sound and fury, signifying nothing.'

27: Or Dante; 'Abandon hope all ye who enter here'.

28: Fear not though: you now know the worst, and it is not something that must be endured with fortitude, for even though all good things must come to an end, Existence is still glorious, and is there to be experienced, and explored, and enjoyed; and for as long as time lasts, you will have God as 'Everything that is' to keep you company.

29: And you have your Earth, which will itself outlast you, and can indeed be regarded in some sense as your God.

30: It is, as you are, a living, breathing organism, with constituent parts that make up the whole, and combine together to create a whole that is greater than the sum of its parts.

31: Just as you can consider yourselves combinations of blood and flesh and bone, organs and nervous systems, and symbioses with microbes; and organise those physical functionings into groups, so too you can consider the living Earth as a function of its outer shells and their contents; the lithosphere, atmosphere and oceans, and biosphere.

32: As part of the whole it is part of the One and therefore, as you yourselves are, it can fairly be treated as God.

33: And when it, and you, and all else besides have surrendered to oblivion, it may well be that God as 'Everything that is not' may then order a new Heaven and new earths. You may even have sequential universes.

34: The truth is that God is multifaceted: God as He; the masculine principle, Everything that is, energy and matter and existence; God as She; the Divine feminine, the Discrete Entity, the Universal Consciousness; God as It; Everything that is not, time and space; and God as They; All for One and One for All.

35: And if you want it in a final form; written as mathematics and as Euclid would have it, God moves between the point and the circle:

36: The point is the beginning of Geometry, and the circle, as the most perfect figure, may be considered its end: the point, being indivisible is also immeasurable, and the circle, with its arc, cannot be measured with precision: the dualism of certainty and probability yet again.

37: And to those of you who say this God is too complicated to make sense, and wish to raise your hands in despair, then you can have the truth of a simple Deism, wherein religion can consist of no more and no less than a contemplation and imagining of the power, wisdom, glory, and benignity of the Deity in her Creation.

38: And to those of you who say this God is too much of a sophism to be believable, and wish to bury yourselves in atheism, then that is your choice; but you must also then choose a meaningless universe.

Postscript

If anyone should be so foolish as to treat this as the last word on these matters, and inscribe it on tablets of stone or any other tablets as gospel truth, may they be plagued and cursed with every misfortune mentioned herein.

For those with a mathematical bent the following definition succinctly defines the totality of the universe:

$$H\Psi = E_i\Psi + jE_i\Psi$$

The totality of possibility encompasses all actualities and all non (or imaginary) actualities.

Appendix

Introduction to the Unauthorised Bible

A fuller justification of the original work of which the above is the conclusion.

This, my magnum opus, has been some four years in the writing, and forty years in the gestation.

It is the book I long since intended to write at the end of my life, and yet at the same time it is not, for the book I began to write four years ago is not the book I have before me now. I have changed during the writing, and have been changed by the writing, and obviously and necessarily the book has changed with me. It is also not, at least in terms of the probabilities that constitute existence, and as far as it is possible to calculate, and barring lightning strikes from an enraged deity, quite the end of my life.

It seems to me that the human psyche has some inbuilt need for some form of religion; in its most basic form as a support mechanism for the rites of passage, and most particularly death, in our need for some reassurance that there is something beyond, and this existence is not just 'dust to dust and ashes to ashes'; and in the deeper sense that any ultimate meaning behind existence requires the existence of that Something Other, no matter what particular form It may or may not take. If we desire a set of moral precepts that are not just an arbitrary construction for convenience, invented to smooth the running of social interactions, we cannot have a Universe which is a mere accident: an absolute set of moral laws requires the existence of God.

To believe or not to believe, remains as always the question, but the decision to select one, and either choice is entirely rational, must also determine the source of our moral codes; the atheistic model makes existence an accident and our moral codes, no matter how well constructed, mere artifices.

It also seems to me that the established religions of the world, in that they are too much in disagreement with science and logic, are no longer fit for purpose, and now constitute a serious threat to the survival of both humanity and the planet. We face 'a perfect storm' of the combination of a human population that the Earth is no longer able to sustain, and an increasing such, resource depletion, climate change, and excessive personal consumption by a significant portion of our species, whilst another portion under-consumes and yet has a legitimate desire to join their more fortunate brethren and partake of the feast. As a direct result of human activities our planet is in trouble, and we need technological, political, and religious systems that aid and direct the changes that need to be made, and not act as a block on them.

The target of the present work is the contribution of religious systems to the core problems, both in the sense of their current contribution, which is by and large negative, and in the sense of their theoretical potential, if they are able to return to their foundations, to change their contributions to positive ones.

The arguments of Malthus and Ehrlich on population expansion are, in their essentials, irrefutable, and as a concomitance the injunction in the Occidental tradition to go forth and multiply is sufficient on its own to condemn that orthodox position to damnation. The Oriental tradition is no better, with its own variations on misogyny, and the two act in tandem, whether through ignorance or deliberate intent, to obstruct probable responses to the problem of overpopulation.

Religions, established or otherwise, and insofar as they are designed for a purpose, if they ever were, serve to give a moral framework to human endeavour. But they cannot be antithetical to science, or any other form of rational enquiry. And science needs to work within a moral framework, for without such, it risks the slippery slope that ends in extremis with the Nazi medical experiments. In philosophical terms, the ends, no matter how estimable or desirable, can never be used to justify means that are immoral.

Science may offer a variety of responses which together may constitute a partial solution to the problems we face, but even as a combination they can only be a partial solution, because in addition attitudes and moral positions also need to change. As controls on our population we probably need universal acceptance of contraception, abortion, assisted suicide, euthanasia, etcetera, but that requires women across the world to have the access to the education that too many of them are denied by tradition and 'culture'. We may need to adopt nuclear fission as a far more general means of producing power, accept a widespread use of genetically modified foods to feed our burgeoning population, and build new high-tech forms of land based public transport to get about, but we will also have to change our selfish consumption patterns, both individual and communal, and construct a new political economy.

To give scientific endeavour and enterprise half a chance to succeed in devising the answers we need to halt and turn back our headlong rush towards disaster, we need to have a moral and religious framework that can work alongside science and not hinder it. We also need religion, because it attempts to answer the questions that science cannot, because they are outwith the purview of science, the whys rather than the hows; the purpose of our existence, or the meaning of life, the problems of evil and suffering, and whether there is anything beyond the grave.

And that brings me to what I hope might be a worthwhile contribution to the debate.

My original intention was to attempt to update the Christian Bible, and to make it compatible with modern understandings of physics, biology, and ethics.

I am happy to admit that I came to the writing with a number of pre-determined political positions, biases if you will, and a political agenda, and, at their core, these remain. As far as I am concerned, revelation may be irrational in the sense of being beyond the rational, but it cannot defy observational truth or logic; it cannot be untrue. God is neither male nor female, women are absolutely and completely the spiritual equals of men, and both misogyny and placing women on pedestals are for ignorami. Injustice is abhorrent, as is man's inhumanity to man and other creatures. Above all I have always been driven by what might be regarded as an obsessive love of freedom; I hate censorship, mobs, and people trying to prevent me saying something they do not like: for me, people must be able to be held responsible for their actions, and that personal accountability requires their possession of free will.

I began with the presumption that the authorised canon of the Christian Bible, as we have it, contained some of the most sublime truths ever committed to paper, and much else of value, but also contained a considerable quantity of what could best be described as repetitive dross, an assortment of obscure and incomprehensible pieces, numerous fairy tales, and some pieces which were not only seriously out of date but positively offensive. As far as I was able to determine, this eccentric mix had been approved by a committee of bishops, using a set of texts that had been constructed and redacted to fit a political agenda that would maintain and support an authoritarian and patriarchal system, and at the behest of the Roman Empire in its need for an official version of the new religion which was to replace the old pagan one. Other texts that might have been included, but which did not fit that agenda, were not just excluded but suppressed.

It is a truism to say that if Jesus returned today he would not recognise the religion whose deity he is as having any connection to what he said. The conventional understanding of the change of religious policy of the fourth century Roman Empire is that Christianity conquered that Roman Empire. The truth is that the Empire conquered the religion. The inspired original movement appealed to and was espoused largely by the dispossessed, the women, the poor, and the slaves. After the take-over it became the property of the rich and powerful, and a good career option. It also provided a mechanism for keeping the peasants in order by offering them the crock of gold at the foot of the rainbow, salvation in paradise for all who follow and obey, the ultimate version of jam tomorrow.

It was also my position that much of the tedious, repetitive pseudo-histories of the Old Testament would surely be better replaced with some of the works of the great theologians; Augustine and Aquinas; the mediaeval mystics, the reformers; Luther and Calvin; poets such as Milton, and modern visionaries such as Kahlil Gibran and Martin Luther King, who all had something more useful to say than much of the old had.

It is, of course, committing lese-majeste on a grand scale to presume to interfere with, never mind vandalise, the received Word of God, but, although I grew up with the understanding that the Christian scriptures were indeed just that, I no longer subscribe to that position. I would now maintain that the authors of the works presently compounded into the authorised bible, whoever and whenever they were, may well have been inspired by deep spiritual insight, holders of a hotline to God as it were, but their understanding does not and cannot hold good in perpetuity. God, whomsoever or whatsoever we presume Her, Him, It, or Them to be, may or may not reveal insights, spiritual, political, philosophical, or theological, to particular individuals at particular junctures in history, but since they are transcribed in human language, which itself changes and develops over time, each and every revelation is determined for time and place. And that is only using a linguistic argument; it is in addition impossible for 'the word of God' to be rubbish; so scriptural 'authorities' for the stoning of adulterers and burning of witches or homosexuals can only ever have been the transpositions of human political and cultural desires, beliefs, and requirements onto the person of God; the creation of God in the image of man. The Word of God is neither written scripture, nor a person, but Creation.

The original intention became further modified as I came to the conclusion that the same comments could be applied to most other religious traditions and scriptures. All of the great prophets, gurus, bodhisattvas, messiahs, call them what we will, were all, in the essentials, saying the same thing: there is a universality in what makes a good person and a good citizen, and in the relationship between Creation and the Divine. Their teachings too had, as with Christianity, been subverted, redacted, and vandalised to form the doctrines of the organised, establishment religions. All organised, established religions are dead constructions based on those teachings of the great masters, and probably, though buried by misogyny, mistresses, which were acceptable to, or could be manipulated so to be, by those who perceived there might be some benefit to them in a new religious settlement.

I am now of the firm opinion that the world is now desperately in need of a revision of its religious settlements, and this work might hopefully be a small contribution to such.

The work before me now is therefore a compound of a much wider set of texts than originally intended. What might have been an attempt at a revised Christian Bible, presumptuous enough in itself, has transmogrified itself into an even more presumptuous attempt at a universal scripture. This might be viewed, and possibly with some justification, as an idiosyncratic selection of sundry religious texts, but, within the restrictions imposed by the overall framework, I have tried to make it as inclusive as possible.

My editing of the texts has of necessity been varied in substance, extent and content.

Many of the original texts, transcribed as they were from older oral traditions, contained too much tedious repetition for my taste, and this has been removed: valuable it may have been as an aid to learning in pre-literate eras but it does not make for easy reading. Prophecy in scripture, in the sense of foretelling the future, has invariably been deleted, since what has traditionally passed as prophecy has either been redacted so that future history makes the prophecy self-fulfilling, or the future history has been written to conform to the prophecy; in either case a fraud has been perpetrated, and that is clearly unacceptable.

The treatment of the varying texts used has differed depending upon the originating tradition: from Hinduism, edited selections from the Upanishads have suffered moderate to severe transliteration, the Bhagavad-Gita has been condensed and similarly transliterated, but only a short piece from the Rig-Veda has been included. The Buddhist Sutras and some of Gautama's parables have been similarly edited, condensed, and transliterated, and then compounded into a single book. For Taoism, Lao Tsu's Tao te Ching has primarily been reorganised, with the application of only a light edit and the usual transliteration, and Stoicism, similarly, is represented by a lightly edited and transliterated version of the Meditations of Aurelius.

Sufism, for reasons which will be further developed later, has been treated as a tradition which has developed beyond its parent religion to such an extent, and is so far removed from the fundamentals of that parent religion, that it now has in reality little connection to that parent, even though most Sufis would maintain the connection is still essential: it is to Islam what Gnosticism was to orthodox Christianity. It has been presented here through heavily edited, condensed, and transliterated versions of the works of Jalal al-Din Rumi, Ibn Al Farid, Mulla Sadra, and Omar Khayyam. The Sikh Scriptures have been condensed into a short compound of the theology and some of the parables of Guru Nanak, and the Bahai faith has been represented by a transliterated condensation of the Hidden Words of Baha'U'llah.

Somewhat regrettably room has only been found for short transliterated passages from the Jewish Kabbalah, and the Jain and Shinto scriptures.

Paganism, in terms of both the traditional animistic and shamanistic small scale tribal religions, the modern 'New Age' reconstructions of such, and the Gaia hypothesis have been conflated from a variety of sources into a single text.

The Judaeo-Christian texts have been largely vandalised: the Mosaic laws of the Pentateuch have been conflated into one slim book, and the Old Testament Prophets have been given similar treatment. Pieces from the Apocrypha, the Nag Hammadi and Dead Sea Texts, the Philokalia, and Thomas A'Kempis have been added in; the Synoptics, the Gospel of John and the Epistle of James have been conflated to one and accredited to James, (given we know far more about him than we do of his brother); segments of the Gnostic Gospels have been conflated with exerts from the Pauline Epistles and accredited to the Magdalene; only Ecclesiastes is untouched, and all the rest has been banished. Genesis Chapter One and The Revelation have been replaced with inventions of mine, and Psalms with a selection of hymns with tolerable theological content.

Being somewhat mischievous I have managed to fit in Satan's wonderful speech to the denizens of the nether regions from Paradise Lost, but since I agree with Blake that Milton was of the party of Satan though he did not know it, it has been redacted to the extent that Lucifer is now the hero and Yahweh is the bad guy. The old creation myth of the fall in Genesis had God parking Adam and in Eve in a paradisiacal garden in a state of innocence whereby they knew not the difference between good and evil; in other words, since the knowledge of that difference is what makes us human; Adam and Eve were not so much innocents as mindless golems created solely to massage God's ego. Given that the placing of the luscious fruits of the forbidden knowledge was an irresistible temptation to defy the will of God, and that the consumption of such would make Eve and then Adam actually thereby properly human, and God's punishing them for so doing was therefore ridiculous, then it was Lucifer's persuasion which set them free from the malignant caprice of their fascist Overlord. In the legend it was Lucifer who made us fully human and is thereby obviously the hero or more probably heroine of the tale.

Because I have in sundry places had people say things they clearly did not say in the original, additions of mine to make them say what I think they should have said if they had thought of such, I will admit that I can with some justification be accused of having concocted a fiction. I would respond that much of our classic scriptures contain substantial portions of fiction, which are there because they best serve the illustration of a point, and I am only following in the tradition, and in any case most of the quotations from the 'originators' were written down many years after their demise, and at third or fourth hand at best, and are themselves therefore probably inventions.

The texts have been ordered in what I now consider to be the rough historical date order in which the originals were written, with the obvious exception of the new Genesis.

A variety of relatively modern texts have been included, from some of the Post-Reformation political philosophers: Locke, Paine, Godwin and Wollstonecraft; through poets: Blake, Dostoevsky, Kahlil Gibran, and T.H. White; and on to modern reformers, both political and religious: Carl Jung, Martin Luther King, Krishnamurti and Gurdjieff. This might now be seen as nothing more than an eclectic collection of texts making up a religious anthology, justified only by my personal taste, and dressed up as Scripture, and that position could certainly be considered to be reasonable. I would accept that much more could have been included, but this is indeed a personal work, and I have chosen the texts I have with deliberate intent in an attempt to illustrate my thesis that all the great religious prophets and poets and philosophers were indeed singing from the same hymn sheet.

The one glaring omission is obviously the Koran/Qur'an, and this is not because I have been intimidated by the thought of being targeted by deranged fanatics, but because, uniquely among the classic texts, I have been unable to find anything in it, even redacted, that is worthy of reproduction. In so far as I can determine it is a confused, disordered recapitulation of the Jewish Old Testament with even dafter fairy tales, self contradicting, and reactionary to boot. There are a few hidden gems, but they are not written in a form that is not expressed at least as well elsewhere. The Qur'an is also, far more than any of its competitors, a work specific to its time and place, and in line with the concerns and intentions of its author, primarily a book of law, liturgy, and political economy. In all the other religious systems it is possible to argue that there can be some separation between the political sphere and personal spiritual development, but that is not possible in Islam, which has always claimed to provide a universal coverage of all aspects of human existence. If any are inclined to defend it against such charges I would simply point out that of all the major religious systems, Islam is the only one to have conquered by the sword from the outset. Given that, and my fairly obvious bias against authoritarianism in any form, my position on Islam, which is defined as surrender to the will of God, could be predicted with some ease. If this were more a political than a theological venture my position on orthodox Islam would be more sympathetic, since Islam's demolition of the decadent, and more importantly, ridiculously disputatious later Roman Empire, with its internecine squabbling over obscurantist points of doctrine, resulted in that noxious body being handed its just desserts. In addition the initial tendencies of the Muslim conquerors allowed the other peoples of the book autonomy of worship and political activity in its widest sense, with the only provision that taxes were paid. Nevertheless this is primarily a theological exercise, so the Islamic tradition, insofar as it might care, will therefore have to be content with being represented by and through its influence on Sikhism and the Bahai faith, and, of greater relevance, through its marvellous development into the heterodox vision of the Sufis, which is so different from the orthodox position, be that Sunni or Shia, as to effectively constitute a separate religion, in the same sense that liberal Christianity and Judaism are becoming increasingly disconnected from the fundamentalist and literalist variants.

In the same way, there might be a future for the liberal and humanitarian variants of all our major religious systems, but there is none for fundamentalist fanaticism.

It might in addition be noted that Confucianism is only represented by a short piece from Meng-Tzu (Mencius), with nothing from Kung Fu-tsu (Confucius). There has always been a debate whether the Confucian system can properly be regarded as a religion at all, or whether it is more simply a code of behaviour. In any case it is far too deferential to traditional authority, to caste, and to the rule of those 'born to rule' for my taste. Zoroastianism is also absent, since although it provided the core source for the Judaeo/Christian/Islamic tradition, and still exists as a religion, its dualistic theology is now too archaic to allow it to be appropriately modified to fit with the dualistic theology of the present work.

I have attempted to make what I have written, redacted, or edited, compatible with modern scientific understanding, or at least compatible with my understanding of modern science. Matching up the theology with Darwinian and neo-Darwinian evolution, psychology and behavioural studies, and modern ethics was easy. Attempting to match it up with modern physics, quantum mechanics and relativity, the magic of Einstein, Bohr, Heisenberg, Schrodinger et. al, was much more of a challenge. Whether I have succeeded, to a great or small extent, is for others to judge, but I have had great fun trying.

Since I now hold one form of God to be synonymous with a Universal Consciousness, Existence in Toto, Energy, and both transcendent and immanent, personal and impersonal, and the other form to be synonymous with the Framework, Non-Existence, that which precedes Existence and will remain after Existence is gone, the vast majority of the texts, from whatever source, have been redacted to use gender neutral pronouns for God. He and She, Her and His, have been treated as interchangeable, and both It and They have on occasion crept in. This of course is not entirely surprising since I consider misogyny to be a creed fit only for idiots.

Via an attempt at a personal spiritual statement and history, and in an attempt thereby to figure out what I now am, I began in childhood in Low church Anglicanism, and from late teens onwards moved successively through agnosticism, a flirtation with evangelical Christianity, neo-paganism, a house church Pentecostalism with a neo-Presbyterian theology, and eventually back to Anglicanism, initially conservative but eventually and ever increasingly liberal. I am now some eccentric conglomerate of Hinduism, Taoism, and neo-Paganism, with an admixture of various Christian heresies, notably the Arian and Pelagian variants. Many will no doubt consider me to be a raving lunatic, a nut-case who thinks he has some divine calling to reconstruct religious orthodoxy, but I would respond that most such do not know that they are mad, whereas I do, on the classic grounds that if the world as we know it is sane then I am more than content to be insane. On a parallel theme, if Heaven is full of religious fundamentalists, whether dressed in white and singing alleluias, or wearing beards and burkhas and laying prostrate, I would find the company of such both eternally irritating and boring, so please banish me to join the fallen women and the lawyers in Hell. I trust I make no such grand claim as presuming to be a prophet; I claim nothing more than that I might be a half-decent editor, and I hope that those, far greater than I, whose works I have modified are content with my revisions.

So why should you read on? If you are interested in the problems of suffering and evil, and whether life has any ultimate meaning, then these texts attempt, to a greater or lesser extent, to give answers. Whether they have succeeded or not is for you to determine. (There is a presumption of course that you have something resembling an open mind, you are open to the potential of enlightenment; if you are committed to a particular position on faith, then you are not open to the possibility that your views might need to be changed.) This work is also intended to educate; it hopefully might provide an introduction to texts and traditions hitherto unknown to the reader, and thereby maybe encourage an investigation of the originals.

Does a Universal Scripture imply a new religion? The answer is both yes and no. Yes in the sense that a Universal Scripture, being inclusive, tolerant and liberal, seeks to replace Scriptures which are too often exclusive, intolerant and illiberal, and even where that is not the case, the religious structures that have grown out of tolerant Scriptures and have ended up being intolerant. An understanding of our proper place in the order of things, and our essential unity with all things, should lead to a better 'care' for that order. And yet it is also no in the sense that religious formalism, being a completely superfluous construct, is anathema to freedom. The old rule is still the new rule: do what thou wilt shall be the whole of the law. There is a corollary though: accept any consequences of your decisions and choices, and to use the vernacular, don't complain if they come back and bite you in the ass. And it is also no in the sense that understanding God as a Universal Consciousness of which we and the whole of existence are part of means that the concept of worship is something of a nonsense: worshipping ourselves would count as hubris of the highest order, worshipping the influenza virus would be eccentric even by my standards, and worshipping the whole is just unnecessary.

A work such as this is, of course, never complete, but there comes a time when it is right to publish, or , alternatively, to 'publish and be damned', and by accepting such, I am also accepting that what I have produced is already out of date and hence ripe for further revision. Part of the problem with orthodox 'scriptures' is that they have been fixed in perpetuity by those who wish to use them to control both other people and the pace of change They are therefore doomed from the start in their primary intent of educating and enlightening, which I hope this work is not.

Bibliography for the Unauthorised Bible

Commentaries

Primary

Dark Nature, Lyall Watson, Hodder and Stoughton, 1995;

The Death of Forever: A New Future for Human Consciousness, Darryl Reanney, Souvenir Press, 1995;

The Garden of Truth, Seyyed Hossein Nasr, Harper Collins, 2008;

The Gnostic Gospels, Elaine Pagels, Phoenix Orion, 2006;

Conversations with God, Neale Donald Walsch, Hodder and Stoughton, 1997;

The Mind of Light, Sri Aurobindo, Lotus Press, 2003;

New Earth, Eckhart Tolle, Penguin Books, 2005;

The Laughing Jesus, Timothy Freke and Peter Gandy, O Books, 2006;

The Gospel of the Second Coming, Timothy Freke and Peter Gandy, Hay House, 2007.

Anthologies

The New Rights of Man, Ed. Jon E. Lewis, Constable and Robinson, 2003;

Applied Ethics, Oxford Readings in Philosophy, Ed. Peter Singer, Oxford University Press, 1987;

The World Treasury of Modern Religious Thought, Ed. Jaroslav Pelikan, Little, Brown and Co., 1990;

Pears Encyclopaedia of Myths and Legends, Ed. Mary Barker and Christopher Cook, Book Club Associates, 1976;

The Concise Encyclopedia of Living Faiths, Ed. R. C. Zaehner, Hutchinson, 1971;

The Concise Encyclopaedia of Islam, Cyril Glasse, Stacey International, 2008;

Man's Religious Quest, Ed. Whitfield Fay, Croom Helm Open University Press, 1982;

The Oxford Dictionary of Quotations, Oxford University Press, 1981.

Biological Sciences

Revenge of Gaia, James Lovelock, Allen Lane, 2006;

The Rise and Fall of the Third Chimpanzee, Jared Diamond, Radius, 1991;

Origins, Richard E. Leakey and Roger Lewin, Book Club Associates, 1977;

Origins Reconsidered, Richard E. Leakey and Roger Lewin, Little, Brown and Co. 1992;

The Origin of Humankind, Richard Leakey, Weidenfield and Nicolson, 1994;

The End of Evolution, Dinosaurs, Mass Extinctions and Biodiversity, Peter Ward, Weidenfield and Nicolson, 1995;

The Holocene: An Environmental History, Neil Roberts, Blackwell, 1998;

Evolution: A Biological and Palaeontological Approach, Ed. Peter Skelton, Addison Wesley, 1996;

The New Sexual Revolution, Robert Pool, Hodder and Stoughton, 1994;

The Darwin Wars, Andrew Brown, Simon and Schuster, 1999.

Combined Sciences

The Creative Cosmos, Ervin Laszlo, Floris Books, 1993;

Laboratory Earth, Stephen H. Schneider, Weidenfield and Nicolson, 1996;

Ubiquity, Mark Buchanan, Weidenfield and Nicolson, 2000;

The Intelligent Universe, Fred Hoyle, Michael Joseph, 1983;

The Knowledge and the Power, Ivan Tolstoy, Canongate Publishing, 1990;

Supernature, Lyall Watson, Coronet Books, 1974;

Comparative Religious Studies

Celtic and Scandinavian Religions, J. A. MacCulloch, Constable, 1994;

The Anthropology of Evil, Ed. David Parkin, Basil Blackwell, 1986;

Celt, Druid and Culdee, Isabel Hill Elder, Covenant Publishing, 1973;

The Age of Fable, Thomas Bullfinch, Harper and Row, 1966.

Historical Studies

The Christian Tradition: A History of the Development of Doctrine, Jaroslav Pelikan, University of Chicago Press, 1971;

James the Brother of Jesus, Robert Eisenman, Watkins Publishing, 2002;

Paul and Hellenism, Hyam Maccoby, SCM Press, 1991;

A Cloud of Witnesses, David N. Bell, Cistercian Publications, 1989;

Centuries of Darkness, Peter James, Pimlico, 1992;

Testament: The Bible and History, John Romer, Michael O'Mara Books, 1989;

The Faith: A History of Christianity, Brian Moynahan, Pimlico, 2003;

The Essene Odyssey, Hugh Schonfield, Element Books, 1985;

The Dead Sea Scrolls Deception, Michal Baigent and Richard Leigh, Jonathan Cape, 1991;

The Jesus Mystery, Lena Einhorn, Lyons Press, 2007;

The Jesus Dynasty, James D. Tabor, Harper Element, 2006;

Jesus of Nazareth: King of the Jews, Paula Fredriksen, Macmillan, 2000;

Hebrew Religion: Its Origin and Development, W. O. E. Oesterley and T. E. Robinson, SPCK, 1930;

The Gifts of the Jews, Thomas Cahill, Nan A. Talese, Bantam Doubleday Bell, 1998;

The Harlot by the Side of the Road: Forbidden Tales of the Bible, Jonathan Kirsch, Rider Books Random House, 1997;

The Destruction of the Jews, Flavius Josephus, Trans. G. A. Williamson, The Folio Society, 1971;

The Great Arab Conquests, Hugh Kennedy, Weidenfield and Nicolson, 2007;

The Trouble with Islam, Irshad Manji, Mainstream Publishing, 2004;

What Went Wrong? The Clash between Islam and Modernity, Bernard Lewis, Weidenfield and Nicolson, 2002;

A History of God, Karen Armstrong, Heinemann, 1992;

Religion in Ancient History, S. G. F. Brandon, George Allen and Unwin, 1969;

A History of Religion East and West, Trevor Ling Macmillan Press, 1982;

The Great Transformation: The World in the time of Buddha, Socrates, Confucius and Jeremiah, Karen Armstrong, Atlantic Books, 2006;

Catastrophe: the Origins of the Modern World, David Keys, Book Club Associates, 1999;

Collapse: How Societies Choose to Fail or Survive, Jared Diamond, Allen Lane, 2005;

Power and Greed, Philippe Gigantes, Constable and Robinson, 2003;

Original Sin, A Cultural History, Alan Jacobs, SPCK, 2008;

A History of Sin, Oliver Thomson, Canongate Press, 1993;

Massacre at Montsegur, Zoe Oldenbourg, Weidenfield and Nicolson, 1997;

The Mysteries of Eleusis, Goblet D'Alviella, The Aquarian Press, 1981;

The New View Over Atlantis, John Michell, Thames and Hudson, 1983.

Literature

The Oxford Shakespeare, Ed. W. J. Craig, Oxford University Press, 1966;

Paradise Lost: The Portable Milton, Ed. Douglas Bush, Penguin Books, 1981;

Ecclesiazusae, Aristophanes, Trans. Jack Lindsay, Complete Aristophanes, Ed. Moses Hadas, Bantam Books, 1971;

The Divine Comedy, Dante Alighieri, J. M. Scott, Heron Books, J. M. Dent, undated;

Faust, Goethe, Trans. Louis Leibrich, Heron Books, J. M. Dent, undated;

Walden, Henry David Thoreau, Folio Society, 1980;

The Book of Merlyn, Thomas Hanbury White, Book Club Associates, 1978;

Hadrian the VII, Frederick Baron Corvo, Wordsworth Editions, 1993;

Alice's Adventures in Wonderland and Through the Looking Glass, Lewis Carroll, Oxford University Press, 1971;

Alice in Quantumland, Robert Gilmore, Copernicus Springer-Verlag, 1995;

Figures of Earth, James Branch Cabell, Wildside Press, 2001;

The Cream of the Jest, James Branch Cabell, Ballantine Books, 1972;

The Silver Stallion, James Branch Cabell, Ballantine Books, 1972;

Jurgen, James Branch Cabell, Dover Publications, 1977;

Stranger in a Strange Land, Robert Heinlein, New English Library, 1982;

Sirius, Olaf Stapledon, Penguin Books, 1973;

Black Easter or Faust Aleph-Null, James Blish, Penguin Books, 1972;

Sartor Resartus, Thomas Carlyle, J. M. Dent, 1973;

Gospel of the Flying Spaghetti Monster, Bobby Henderson, Harper Collins, 2006.

Philosophy

God and Philosophy, Anthony Flew, Hutchinson and Co., 1968;

Philosophy of Religion, Fulton J. Sheen, Browne and Nolan Ltd., 1952;

The Future of Man, Pierre Teilhard de Chardin, Trans. Norman Denny, Collins, 1964;

The Principle of Duty, David Selbourne, Sinclair-Stevenson, 1994;

Practical Ethics, Peter Singer, Cambridge University Press, 1993;

Seven Theories of Human Nature, Leslie Stevenson, Oxford University Press, 1981;

The Quest for Meaning, Oswald Hanfling, Open University, Basil Blackwell, 1987;

The Mind of God, Paul Davies, Simon and Schuster, 1992;

Beginning Lives, Rosalind Hursthouse, Open University, Basil Blackwell, 1987;

Ending Lives, Robert Campbell and Diane Collinson, O. U., Basil Blackwell, 1987;

Irrationality, The Enemy Within, Stuart Sutherland, Constable and Co., 1992;

Intellectuals, Paul Johnson, Weidenfield and Nicolson, 1988

The Subjection of Women, John Stuart Mill, Ed. Susan M. Okin, Hackett Publishing, 1988;

Causing Death and Saving Lives, Jonathan Glover, Penguin Books, 1986;

Principles of Biomedical Ethics, Tom L. Beauchamp and James F. Childress, Oxford University Press, 1983;

The Reason of Things, A. C. Grayling, Weidenfield and Nicolson, 2003;

Metaphysics as a Guide to Morals, Iris Murdoch, Vintage, 2003;

Reasons and Persons, Derek Parfit, Clarendon Press, 1987;

Straw Dogs, Thoughts on Humans and Other Animals, John Gray, Granta Publications, 2003;

Unended Quest, Karl Popper, Fontana, 1986;

Jurisprudence, J. G. Riddall, Anthony Rowe Ltd, 1996;

The Proper Study of Mankind, Isaiah Berlin, Pimlico, 1998;

Voltaire's Bastards, John Ralston Saul, Sinclair-Stevenson, 1992;

The Ethics of Aristotle, Trans. J. A. K. Thomson, Penguin, 1984;

The Republic of Plato, Trans. Francis M. Cornford, Oxford University Press, 1961;

Essays, Michel de Montaigne, Trans. E. J. Trechmann, Oxford University Press, 1927;

The Essential Descartes, Ed. Margaret D. Wilson, Meridian Books, 1983;

Pensees, Blaise Pascal, Trans. Honor Levi, Oxford University Press, 1995;

Critique of Pure Reason, Immanuel Kant, Trans. J.M.D. Meiklejohn, Dover Publications, 2003,

The Ethics, Benedict de Spinoza, Trans. R. H. M. Elwes, Constable and Co. 1955;

Philosophical Works, George Berkeley, J. M. Dent, 1985;

Philosophical Writings, Gottfried Leibniz, J. M. Dent, 1973;

The Social Contract, Jean-Jacques Rousseau, Trans Maurice Cranston, Penguin, 1968;

Twilight of the Idols and The Anti-Christ, Friedrich Nietzsche, Trans. R. J. Hollingdale, Penguin Books, 1981.

Physical Sciences

The Holographic Universe, Michael Talbot, Grafton Books, 1991;

About Time, Einstein's Unfinished Revolution, Paul Davies, Viking, 1995;

The Last Three Minutes, Paul Davies, Weidenfield and Nicolson, 1994;

The Origin of the Universe, John D. Barrow, Weidenfield and Nicolson, 1994;

The Matter Myth, Paul Davies and John Gribbin, Viking, 1991;

The Mind Matters: Consciousness and Choice in a Quantum World, David Hodgson, Clarendon Press, 1993;

The Character of Physical Law, Richard Feynman, The MIT Press, 1992;

The Mystery of the Quantum World, Euan Squires, Adam Hilger Ltd, 1986;

The World Treasury of Physics, Astronomy and Mathematics, Ed. Timothy Ferris, Little, Brown and Co., 1991.

Politics and Economics

The Road to Serfdom, F. A. Hayek, Routledge and Kegan Paul, 1976;

Law, Legislation and Liberty, F. A. Hayek, Routledge and Kegan Paul, 1979;

Good Work, E. F. Schumacher, Jonathan Cape, 1979;

Human Scale, Kirkpatrick Sale, Secker and Warburg, 1980;

The Breakdown of Nations, Leopold Kohr, Green Books, 2001;

The Origins of Totalitarianism, Hannah Arendt, George Allen and Unwin, 1967;

The Open Society and Its Enemies, Karl Raimond Popper, Routledge and Kegan Paul, 1993;

The Future of Freedom, Fareed Zakaria, W.W. Norton and Co., 2003;

Free to Choose, Milton and Rose Friedman, Secker and Warburg, 1980;

Man and Society, John Plamenatz, Longman, 1993;

An Essay on the Principle of Population, Thomas R. Malthus, J. M. Dent, 1973;

This Land is Our Land, Marion Shoard, Paladin Grafton Books, 1987;

Deschooling Society, Ivan Illich, Calder and Boyars, 1974;

Earth in the Balance, Al Gore, Earthscan Publications, 1994;

How to Save the World, The Politics of Scale, Ed. Nicholas Albery and Yvo Peeters, Fourth World Educational Trust, 1982;

The Thomas Paine Reader, Ed. Michael Foot and Isaac Kramnick, Penguin Books, 1987;

Leviathan, Thomas Hobbes, Penguin, 1982.

Scriptures

Sacred Texts of the World, Ed. Ninian Smart and Richard D. Hecht, Quercus, 1982;

The Epic of Gilgamesh, Penguin Books, 1980;

Judaism, The Tanakh, The New JPS Translation, Ed Jaroslav Pelikan, Quality Paperback Book Club, 1992;

Holy Bible, New King James Version, Thomas Nelson, 1980;

The Jerusalem Bible, Ed. Alexander Jones, Darton, Longman and Todd, 1974;

The New English Bible: Apocrypha, Oxford and Cambridge University Press, 1970;

The Rig Veda, Trans. Wendy O'Flaherty, Penguin Books, 1981;

The Upanishads, Trans. Juan Mascaro, Penguin Books, 1979;

Hindu Scriptures, Trans. And Ed. Dominic Goodall, Phoenix Press, 2005;

The Song of God: Bhagavad-Gita, Trans. Swami Prabhavananda and Christopher Isherwood, Phoenix House, 1967;

A Study of the Siva Sutras: Finding the Hidden Self, Roger Worthington, Himalayan Institute Press, 2002;

The Kama Sutra, Trans. Richard Burton, Book Club Associates, George Allen and Unwin, 1980;

Tao Te Ching, Lao-Tzu, Trans. Stephen Mitchell, Kyle Cathie, 1990;

The Analects of Confucius and the Sayings of Mencius, Trans. James Legge, Signature Press, 2008;

Buddhist Scriptures, Trans. Edward Conze, Penguin Books, 1981;

Buddhist Parables, Anon., Axiom Publishing, 2009;

The Book of Jasher, Trans. Flaccus Albinus Alcuinus, The Rosicrucian Order, 1979;

The Lost Books of the Bible, Trans. William Hone, Testament Books, 1979;

The Nag Hammadi Scriptures, Trans. and Ed. Marvin Meyer, Harper Collins, 2008;

The Lost Sutras of Jesus, Trans. Jon Babcock, Ed. Ray Riegert and Thomas Moore, Souvenir Press, 2004;

Metamorphoses, Ovid, Trans. John Dryden, Wordsworth Editions, 1998;

The Koran, Trans. N. J. Dawood, Allen Lane, 1978;

The Holy Qur'an, Trans. Abdullah Yusuf Ali, Wordsworth Editions, 2000;

The Book of Urizen, William Blake, Thames and Hudson, 1979;

The Rubaiyat of Omar Khayyam, Edward Fitzgerald, Ed. George F. Maine, Collins, 1972;

The Prophet, Kahlil Gibran, Book Club Associates, 1978.

Spirituality

Denial of the Soul, Spiritual and Medical Perspectives on Euthanasia and Mortality, M. Scott Peck, Simon and Schuster, 1997;

The Last Hours of Ancient Sunlight, Thom Hartmann, Hodder and Stoughton, 1999;

The Fruitful Darkness, Joan Halifax, Grove Press, 1993;

The Spiritual Teachings of Marcus Aurelius, Mark Forstater, Hodder and Stoughton, 2001;

The Spiritual Teachings of Seneca, Mark Forstater and Victoria Radin, Hodder and Stoughton, 2001;

Living Beauty, Ways of Mystical Prayer, Oliver Davies, Darton, Longman and Todd, 1990;

The Dalai Lama's Book of Wisdom, Ed. Matthew E. Bunson, Rider Books, 1997;

Powers Within, Selections from the Works of Sri Aurobindo and Mirra Alfassa, The Mother, A. S. Dalal, Lotus Press, 2007;

Hayakal al-Nur, The Shape of Light, Hazrat Shihabuddin Yahya al-Suhrawardi, Int. Shaykh Tosun Bayrak al-Jerrahi al-Halveti, Fons Vitae, 2006;

An Owner's Manual for the Human Being, Michael Gilbert, Samuel Weiser Inc., 1980;

Operation Redemption, George Trevelyan, Turnstone Press, 1981;

The Tibetan Book of Living and Dying, Sogyal Rinpoche, Random House, 1993;

The Monastic Journey, Thomas Merton, Sheldon Press, 1977;

Eternal Echoes, John O'Donohue, Bantam Books, 2000;

The Elements of a Spiritual Life, F. P. Harton, SPCK, 1939;

Christian Spirituality: Post Reformation and Modern, Ed. Louis Dupre and Don E. Saliers, SCM Press, 1989;

The Mystical Christ, Manly P. Hall, Philosophical Research Society, 1975;

The Power of Now, Eckhart Tolle, Hodder and Stoughton, 2005.

Theology

Summa Theologiae, St. Thomas Aquinas, A Concise Translation, Ed. Timothy McDermott, Methuen, 1991;

City of God, Augustine, Trans. Henry Bettenson, Penguin Books, 1981;

St. Anselm's Proslogion, Trans. M. J. Charlesworth, University of Notre Dame Press, 1979;

The Synoptic Gospels, H. A. Guy, Macmillan Education, 1985;

The Gnostic Gospels, Elaine Pagels, Phoenix Orion Books, 2006;

The Gospel of Mary of Magdala, Karen L. King, Polebridge Press, 2003;

The Voice, The Word, The Books, F. E. Peters, Princeton University Press, 2007;

The People of the Book?: The Authority of the Bible in Christianity, John Barton, SPCK, 1988;

An Introduction to the Books of the Apocrypha, W.O. E. Oesterley, SPCK, 1953;

Introduction to the New Testament, A. H. McNeille, Oxford University Press, 1953;

On Religion: Speeches to its Cultured Despisers, Friedrich Schleiermacher, Trans. John Oman, Harper Torchbooks, 1958;

Fear and Trembling, Soren Kierkegaard, Trans Alastair Hannay, Penguin Books, 1985;

An Interpretation of Christian Ethics, Reinhold Niebuhr, Seabury Press, 1979;

Elements of Moral Theology, R. C. Mortimer, Adam and Charles Black, 1947;

Faith, Louis Jacobs, Valentine, Mitchell and Co., 1968;

The Church, Hans Kung, Trans. Ray and Rosaleen Ockenden, Search Press, 1986;

The Church with a Human Face, Edward Schillebeeckx, Trans. John Bowden, SCM Press, 1985;

Theology, Church and Ministry, John Macquarrie, SCM Press, 1986;

Subject and Object in Modern Theology, James Brown, SCM Press, 1953;

A Pattern of Faith: An Exposition of Christian Doctrine, Geoffrey Paul, Churchman Publishing, 1986;

Connections: The Integration of Theology and Faith, J. L. Houlden, SCM Press, 1986;

A God Who Acts, Harry Blamires, SPCK, 1981;

Jesus in Our Western Culture, Edward Schillebeeckx, Trans. John Bowden, SCM Press, 1987;

Metaphysics and the Idea of God, Wolfhart Pannenberg, Trans. Philip Clayton, T. & T. Clark, 1990;

The Anachronism of Time, Iain Mackenzie, Canterbury Press, 1994;

Space, Time and Resurrection, Thomas F. Torrance, Handsel Press, 1976;

Religion and Science, Conflict and Synthesis, Ian T. Ramsey, S.P.C.K. 1964;

One World: The Interaction of Science and Theology, John Polkinghorne, SPCK, 1986;

To Care for the Earth, Sean McDonagh, Cassell Publishers, 1988;

The End of Ancient Christianity, Robert Markus, Cambridge University Press, 1990;

The Mysticism of the Cloud of Unknowing, William Johnston, Anthony Clarke, 1987;

Reincarnation: The Missing Link in Christianity, Elizabeth Clare Prophet; Summit University Press, 1997;

Digest of the Divine Law, Howard B. Rand, Destiny Publishers, 1959;

The Secret History of Lucifer, Lynn Picknett, Constable and Robinson, 2005;

Gods of the Earth, Michael Jordan, Bantam Press, 1992;

The Gospel of Barnabas, David Sox, George Allen and Unwin, 1984;

Jesus the Master Builder, Druid Mysteries and the Dawn of Christianity, Gordon Strachan, Floris Books, 1999;

God, Alexander Waugh, Review Headline Book Publishing, 2002.

Sundries

Getting a Life, Polly Ghazi and Judy Jones, Hodder and Stoughton, 1997;

Pronoia is the Antidote for Paranoia, Rob Brezsny, Frog Ltd., 2005;

Introductory Lectures on Psycho-Analysis, Sigmund Freud, Trans. Joan Riviere, Heron Books, George Allen and Unwin, undated;

Godel, Escher, Bach: An Eternal Golden Braid, Douglas R. Hofstadter, Penguin Books, 1979;

The Golden Bough, Sir James George Frazer, Macmillan and Co., 1923;

Magick, Aleister Crowley, Ed. John Symonds and Kenneth Grant, Routledge and Kegan Paul, 1985.

SD - #0044 - 060826 - C0 - 216/138/9 - PB - 9781780350530 - Gloss Lamination